NO ORDINARY
FAMILY

No Ordinary Family

A Sisterhood in Softball

Kelbe Callaway shows why she is a determined
ballplayer as she connects for the Playmakers.

Robert A. Jackson

authorHOUSE®

AuthorHouse™ LLC
1663 Liberty Drive
Bloomington, IN 47403
www.authorhouse.com
Phone: 1-800-839-8640

Published by AuthorHouse   11/05/2013

ISBN: 978-1-4918-2381-1 (sc)
ISBN: 978-1-4918-2058-2 (hc)
ISBN: 978-1-4918-2380-4 (e)

Library of Congress Control Number: 2013918073

CONTENTS

INTRODUCTION

Some might question the logic of writing this book, but I have rarely been accused of being logical or sensible.

Mostly, I am a contrarian that likes to rage against the machine.

The young ladies that make up the softball team known as the Arkansas Playmakers, their families, their coaches and their attitudes are unique in my opinion - and that is what attracted me to their story.

Usually, all-star, select or travel teams composed of athletes that compete apart from organized high or middle school athletics are composed of extremely talented youngsters that come together to win and perhaps catch the eye of a college coach with the anticipation that an athletic scholarship will be the end result of the entire process. Apart from the game, they are strangers to each other.

These all-star or special teams often recruit athletes or youngsters who come from families that are able to pay significant sums of money to cover the cost of private coaches and travel expenses. And as I said, their ability to stand out and play sports like baseball, softball or soccer is the only tie the players have with each other on the team.

Local Little League, Pop Warner, Babe Ruth as well as county-based recreational organizations are designed to offer athletic opportunities to the general public and youngsters in a neighborhood setting. Playing the game and learning about sportsmanship is the real purpose behind what they offer. The players know each other, hang out together and grow up as friends; while the parents often work at the same company, live in the same neighborhood and share good times together.

The Playmakers seem to have a foot in both continents.

The team was formed by parents that felt their young girls were not getting the best coaching or were not being offered the best opportunity to develop their talents within the local recreational softball programs operating across Ashley County, Arkansas.

The parents of the original Playmaker squad also wanted more control of the situation and they wanted their daughters to be on teams with more talent than could be found in the community-based recreational programs in the county's smaller towns.

However, the hiring of private coaches and pushing their daughters toward a level that would result in college scholarships was not in their world view.

They wanted to go beyond southeastern Arkansas for competition and experience, but they also wanted to keep their team grounded in the values of rural Arkansas. The parents would still coach them and the girls would always be proud of their hometowns and the people they call neighbors.

Until the girls were old enough to join their county high school teams, Playmaker parents set up a schedule of weekend travel and tournaments that lasted from late winter - and early spring - into autumn.

They also wanted to maintain a sense of family, therefore the girls morphed from teammates into sisters. It is not surprising to find that after eight years, six of the team's original 10 team members are still with the team and three others have been Playmakers for at least three seasons - one of that trio is in her fourth.

There is no pay to play, private coaching or scholarship hunting in the Playmaker playbook.

What is in their manual are unique values that go beyond excellence on the field.

Instead of doing whatever it takes to win, recruiting new players to make the team better while letting go those that fail to measure up and a hectic travel schedule, the Playmakers have chosen to maintain a base of players.

The parents also chose to pass up tournaments that could bring a lot more attention in favor of staying within a more family-based association such as Babe Ruth ball.

Until the last couple of years, in major Babe Ruth league sanctioned tournaments players travelling far from their hometowns were required to stay with host families from the community that was hosting the tournament. Staying in expensive or even modest hotels and motels was not allowed.

Many of the Playmaker players still remember their host families that provided a home to them when travelling to, and playing in, out of state tournaments. They also still retain close bonds with the children of those families, bonds that turned them into cousins; and the players from opposing teams they met in those tournaments held in Texas, Mississippi, Louisiana and Colorado remain good friends.

Is there any drama?

No, said Bobby Livingston - the father of one of the original Playmakers.

"They've pretty much been raised Christian," he explained. "We have a Sunday morning devotional when we are on road. (Coach) Johnny (Pierce) has a pre-game prayer with them before each game."

But what really convinced me that writing this book on the Playmakers was the right way to spend my free time away from work as a reporter was what Katie Koen wrote following a tournament championship game in Benton during the team's final season together in 2013.

Koen is about 5-7, smiles a lot, thinks her boyfriend is super and is about as normal as any country-born teen-ager despite the fact that she is a softball player with plenty of talent.

She also has plenty of personality, has a warm heart and is very gregarious.

I asked her to help with this book and what follows were her recollections of a post-game gathering after a Playmaker tournament win over a team known as Nitro.

"There are several of the girls on the Nitro team that I have grown close to over the years. At the end of every game, both teams meet at the pitcher's mound to say the Lord's Prayer. Typically, a couple of girls draw crosses in the dirt on the mound. I usually don't pay that much attention; however, this time I noticed that the Nitro's Emily Law was writing letters. She wrote DM on the mound along with the cross.

"I knew what it meant the moment it happened and I started crying. One of my former teammates from Benton *(Koen played on the Benton-based Hustle before joining the Playmakers),* Drew Melton, was tragically killed in a car accident in November 2012. Between the first and second game (of the Benton tournament), my parents and I drove to the crash site. My dad wanted me to see the results of a poor decision. In addition, we happened to be playing on one of the fields I used to practice with her. She had been on my mind all day long.

"After the prayer and hugs, I asked Emily how she knew Drew. She told me she had never personally met her; but, had played against her growing up."

Before finishing my review of Katie's writing, I have to say that the Playmakers had just nipped Nitro for a summer tournament title. It was a close game and after the contest, the Nitro coach yelled in an angry tone, "We will see you next week . . . we are going to work all week and we will get you." He also directed some language at a Playmaker coach that I would rather leave out, except to say that it was not pleasant.

Now back to Katie.

"It means a lot to me when I see the kind of impact we all have on each other. I know at least a couple of people on every team and have played against almost all of them at some point in my life . . . not only do you get a competitive environment to play ball, you make lifelong friends and impact lives. Drew will never be forgotten and I am honored to have had the chance to play with her when I did."

In athletic activities competition can get heated, but if you get to know Katie, Kelbe Callaway, Destiny Bolen, Jada Wilson and all of the other Playmakers you will learn that while losing is unacceptable to them, the most important element is living and living life well; and that includes family and lifelong friendships.

Makenzie Pierce looks back toward home plate after reaching second base.

Kelbe Callaway, Makenzie Pierce, Aubree Head and Bre Smith come together during a break in a tournament in Mississippi.

Jada Wilson plays third base.

INNING ONE

Not every book or article about a team has to be about a championship run, the end of a dynasty or a cultural or anthropological study.

Books or serious publications examining high school football in Texas or Ohio or Georgia have their place just as pro league tell all diaries; however, that should not be the only way to write about the sporting world or youth athletics.

Sometimes, a simple book about a simple team in a small town can be allowed on the bookshelves alongside a tome on the great American pastime of high school or college football.

In the rural southeastern corner of Arkansas I have found a story that I thought could only be found in Hollywood; well, the Hollywood of the Golden Era. Something in the tale seemed too good to be true; but fortunately it was true.

This is the story of a small group of young girls, their parents and a town that has adopted them.

These girls have found that being a team is more important than being individual stars. They are loyal to their communities. They have become a family and they simply love to play softball.

The girls are called the Arkansas Playmakers; and they are the subject of this book.

Friendship among families, heartbreak, youngsters being youngsters, daughters and that special tie that they have with their Dads - and the joy that comes with finally winning the big game - are subjects of the story that is the Arkansas Playmakers.

Yes, life is rough; but the reality that is life does not have to be what we view on raunchy and somewhat obscene TV reality shows.

The Arkansas Playmakers have a real story to tell. It is not, "Father Knows Best" or "Happy Days"; nor, is it "Dance Moms" or "Hell's Kitchen." It is definitely not "Friday Night Lights."

This is not a soap opera or a book about romance or scandal. I am not going to make every at bat a moment of high drama or overplay the normal hiccups in life faced by 16 or 17 year old young ladies.

This story is about what makes the Playmakers a special group of young ladies - a rare story of winners on the field and away from the park. Yes, they have won trophies and they win a lot of them; yet, the team is a winner because of who the girls are and who their parents are and their brothers and sisters. In and of themselves the girls, their families and parents are ordinary.

There is nothing wrong with being ordinary. There is something to be proud about when you work 40 plus hours in a week, bring home an honest paycheck as a mother or a father and are there for your children. There is something to be proud about when you go to class, share laughs with friends, enjoy athletics, tease teammates and share special moments with one's brother or sister.

No greedy agents or players, no obnoxious fans or a win at any cost attitude can be found in the world of the Playmakers.

"I've been fortunate," Coach Todd Callaway said. "I've had a good group of girls."

OK, a motel door may have been broken, tears of joy and disappointment shed and learning hard lessons in life at too early an age may have taken place; however, the creation of a family that shares special moments is as important a story as any high-priced soaper or modern-day tell-all filled with drugs, sex and abusive parents.

There are still stories in sport that tell the story of team and family. This is one of those stories. This is a story about Aubree, Miss Lissa, Kenzie, Kelbe, JadaBo and Destiny (D Bo to her coaches). It is a story of fathers and daughters. It is a tale about a brother and his twin sister - and her friends. It is a story about long drives. It is about Katie, Ashleigh and Kayla. It is a story about a week in Colorado.

This is a story about the family I call the Arkansas Playmakers.

There are several ways to begin the Playmakers' tale, but perhaps the best place to start is in the suburban hamlet called Sherwood - just outside Little Rock, Ark.

But before I begin, there were words spoken during a post-practice gathering during the final season of Playmaker play - the summer of 2013.

Kelbe Callaway wanted to make a point. She said the best way to ruin any relationship with her is to tell her she played well and to pat her on the back after a loss.

"I don't like (to lose); I don't like it at all."

Point made and the point was taken.

But then a voice came from the back corner of the dugout.

"I hate to lose more than I like to win."

The voice was the high-pitched voice of the team's primary catcher - little Makenzie Pierce.

At 5-4, Pierce does not look at all like the dirt devil she is on the diamond. Pierce is a dark haired beauty with a quiet charm. She doesn't say a lot, but when she feels like it Pierce will tell you how she feels.

She also knows just about everything there is to know about playing behind the plate. Ask her a question about being a catcher and she not only has the answer but the why to go with it. For example, she explained to me why it is simply irrational for a catcher to toss off her mask - a traditional practice - as she or he tries to locate a pop up around home plate.

Callaway is also not shy. You know where you stand when she is in the room.

She is also truly Irish with the reddest of hair and most open of personalities. The Playmaker first baseman nearly always smiles except when she steps up to the plate or handles a low throw. Then you see the focus and intensity in her face.

Georgia may have Scarlet O'Hara; however, I am very fortunate to learn that Southern Arkansas has the amazing Kelbe Callaway holding down the fort at first base.

Callaway will battle until the clock strikes midnight - and the final out is made. However, for Callaway the time is always 10:30 p.m., and there is always plenty of time left to win.

In Sherwood, the words of Callaway and Pierce rang out like a clarion bell in the middle of a dark winter's night.

Unfortunately, for everyone involved it was anything but a winter's night.

It was mid-June 2012. It was a hot summer Saturday. It was a one-day, double-elimination tournament called the Father's Day Classic.

"We didn't show up a lick," Brad Koen, Katie Koen's dad, said. Playmakers chimed in and agreed with him - explaining how the tournament began.

I went back, checked the records and they were right. The Playmakers lost their first game in Sherwood to the Arkansas Force, 6-0.

That did not sit well with Katie, Kelbe or Makenzie.

In the loser's bracket, the Playmakers made rival teams pay for the opening game loss. The team wearing kelly green won four consecutive games by the score of 24-8.

That put the Playmakers back in the semifinal round. The next foe - the Force. Mad, angry, a bit tired and ready for revenge - the Playmakers were not going to lose again. The two teams - the Playmakers and the Force - fought like heavyweights. On the table was a berth in the final match of the day.

Strong play in the field, clutch strikeouts and big hits from both sides marked the contest. Neither the Force nor the Playmakers were going to lose.

Still, the Playmakers survived, 5-4.

The Playmakers had survived and were in the finals.

But, it had been a long ride. Six games had been played and the last of the six was a battle. Toss in the time, it was after midnight when the championship game began, and the Saturday tournament had turned into a true Father's Day Classic. The Playmakers could be excused for choosing to go home, but the team in green chose to stay at least two more hours.

Aubree Head, the team's outfielder and optional infielder, had to be in Tuscaloosa, Al. bright and early Monday morning for a softball camp.

Jada Wilson had spent the days leading up to the Sherwood Tournament playing at a high school all-star game. She returned in time to handle the hot corner and brought with her a very determined attitude. Makenzie spent her week before Sherwood partying with her Hamburg High friends and cheering with an intense focus at a cheerleading camp on the beaches of Florida and in the hot gymnasiums of Panama City.

During the early games of the Sherwood tournament, Head's hand was spiked on a play at second base. Cut and bruised she played on because the 10-player team lost Pierce. Pierce became sick and she was forced into a designated hitter role. A long hot summer's day behind home plate had turned into a very muggy night. Game after game simply wore her down.

Koen was moved from the infield to behind the plate.

I learned while writing this book that Koen is a player with many homes on the diamond. She almost always smiles and jokes. She is also a true athlete who can catch, pitch, play the infield and step up to play any outfield role you ask her to play.

Pierce moved for the final game to the bleachers behind home plate and the backstop. She took cat naps between at-bat opportunities as the Playmaker's designated hitter.

Todd Callaway, coach and Kelbe's dad, said he had forgotten how many games the Playmakers played on that long summer day and night. That statement was made Sunday afternoon, several hours after the team returned home to southeastern Arkansas.

The Playmakers didn't seem to care. For them the only math that is important involves the counting of runs.

The Ferndale Fireballs were ready and waiting in the championship game. It was after midnight and the contest became another classic. But to Kelbe Callaway the clock was still only 10:30 p.m.

Neither team was sharp enough to make many plays, Kelbe admitted. It was sloppy, she explained with a laugh.

The game would be decided by the bats. The Playmakers were out of pitching, but not heart.

Destiny Bolen and Koen each blasted two-run home runs.

Pierce woke up and delivered a clutch two-out hit.

"I don't like to lose," Pierce said.

Then in the 8th inning, Head's bases-loaded double scored two runs, runs that gave the Playmakers a 15-14 win.

The exact time the game ended remains in doubt. Was it 1:30 a.m. or did it last until 3.

Callaway was up and ready for every inning; however, she had to be helped to the car - much like Ali after the Thriller in Manila. And like Ali, she was the winner.

Aubree Head got home, got an hour's worth of sleep before waking up to bandage her hand as she got ready for the drive to Crimson Tide country.

Kelbe and her father got home in time to get three hours of sleep. Sunday was Father's Day and the Callaways never miss church services.

Johnny Pierce let Makenzie get her rest. Why? Sunday practice was mercifully cancelled.

Kayla Livingston sits in front of a welcome home sign put
up in the Town Square of Hamburg in 2011.

Jada Wilson takes a breather.

Makenzie Pierce with her dad Johnny.

INNING TWO

I think I should introduce the final edition of the 2013 Playmakers at this point.

There are the original six, the three later additions and the 10th.

The original six are the six young ladies that came together as seven and eight year-olds, and hung together as a family for eight softball seasons.

Those "original 6" are Jada Wilson, Kelbe Callaway, Makenzie Pierce, Destiny Bolen, Aubree Head and Kayla Livingston.

Wilson is the third baseman, Callaway is at first base, Pierce is the catcher and Bolen handles most of the team's pitching duties. Head, called Bradley by her mother, is a talented infielder; however, her ability to use her long legs to cover plenty of field has her often holding down the fort as an outfielder. Livingston is an outfielder, and the team's quietest of players.

If she were not such a clutch player, you might forget she is a true talent or a member of the team.

The three recruits that joined the team for the last series of seasons were Katie Koen (three seasons), Bre Smith (four) and Ashleigh White (three). The 10th player is usually a player brought in for a season to fill a special need or add a little extra to what the starting nine bring to the table. For the final edition of the Playmakers, the new addition was Avery Barnett.

Barnett was much younger (three years the junior of Katie and Bre) and quieter; however, around friends and family she shows the smile and spunk she displays on the field of play. She is also a talent with big-time potential as a third baseman. Yet, with Wilson on the team; Barnett was standing and making plays out in left field.

Callaway, White, Pierce and Koen are personalities. They bring emotion to the game and are vocal leaders. They also can be devilish at times. When that happens, Jada simply gets a grin and shakes her head as if to say, "What can I do with them."

Head is the back-slapper that is always moving around nervously in the dugout, but she seems to find peace and calmness once she puts on her glove or grabs a bat. A National Honor Society student, Head can be cerebral as a player. However, she constantly demands a lot of herself both mentally and physically.

"She demands a lot of herself," Coach and father Chris Head told me of the girl I call the professor.

He told me that when she gets upset and that look of anger is on her face, no team can stop her from scoring once she gets on base. The same can be said when she is in the field. Rarely do batters get balls past her either at shortstop or in the outfield when Aubree tightens her eyes into a glare.

Her father is equally proud of the triple play she turned in during a high school game or the running catch into the shallow outfield space that most pop flies go to die and hit the ground.

Her running catch as the team's shortstop turned into a dramatic inning-ending double play to help the Playmakers advance toward another title during the summer of 2012.

With Head among the returning players, the 2013 edition of the Playmaker unit was the most mature edition and perhaps the most independent because more of the players were now old enough to drive their own forms of transportation.

The days when the girls could only get to practice and games by depending upon parental units was now gone.

It was June 2013 and the parents that wanted to go to practice and attend games had to drive alone in their own vehicles. The girls brought their gloves, balls and bats in their own vehicles and made it to the ballpark on their own terms. It was a new era for the Playmaker franchise.

After a practice session, Chris Head said he was going to be tied up at his job and could not leave for a 6 p.m. game in distant El Dorado until after 5 p.m. - and he did not expect to arrive at the park until game time. Other parents had similar time issues.

No problem, because the girls were able to arrange car pools among themselves so that they would be at the field in El Dorado early enough for pre-game drills and warm-up activity. Parents and coaches did not have to be there because the girls were old enough - and independent.

Independence is a great thing, but it does bring a certain amount of new responsibility.

Budgeting one's time and making sure that you have all of the tools of the trade with you when you leave for work - well, practice or a game - is now your responsibility. Depending upon mom to handle all of the details was no longer an acceptable option or excuse.

However, there is one thing the girls will never have to worry about - and that one thing is Dad. Dad will always be there.

The bond between a father and son in baseball may be classic, but it has nothing on the Father-Daughter tie that exists in softball.

Daughters in softball are the result of a simple mathematical equation. Daughter plus Dad plus glove and bat divided by time multiplied by miles travelled equal a softball player.

In a **Facebook** post that included a photograph of Kelbe standing at first base with her father in the adjacent coaching box, Kelbe wrote, "The main reason a daughter needs a dad is to show her that not all boys are like the ones who hurt her."

They rarely hug or show emotion, but the Callaways are like the other nine Dads and Daughters that make up the Arkansas Playmakers.

It is impossible to get space between them even if they are miles and hours apart.

The father-daughter relationship is unbreakable.

Where one is, they both are. It sounds like a philosophical proverb uttered by a wise man from China, but it is true.

Kelbe and Todd Callaway are close, and while they may be two individuals there is only one real spirit.

Chris Head is always smiling and joking, but when he tells daughter Aubree to alter her swing, get down so she can smother an infield ground ball or to set her feet before making the throw to first base there is a look of clear determination on his face.

Aubree will always listen and show an understanding when Playmaker Coaches Todd Callaway and Johnny Pierce direct her play; but when her father speaks it is as if Mozart has been told to be a little lighter with his touch on the piano.

She swings from anger to being emotionally frustrated, but if anyone dare tell her that everything is OK and don't worry about what dad has just said I urge you to watch out.

She might turn in a moment's notice from the softball professor to Lizzie Borden with a bat in her hand because she knows that her Dad is simply telling her out loud just what she is thinking quietly and telling herself at the same time with her own inner voice. Clearly, she is reacting to an inner voice that just happens to be coming from her father's outer voice. And no one should doubt or question her Dad.

"I have always had my daddy as a coach, whether he is really on the field, in the dugout or in the stands," she said. "With your dad as a coach, you know no matter what, you are gonna be the one he is the hardest on."

After practice or a game Chris and Aubree talk, finish each other's sentences, kid each other and often communicate via telepathy.

"I love having him out there," she explained.

The relationship between Chris and Aubree is mirrored by the Bolens and ever other Playmaker twosome of Dad and Daughter.

"Her daddy has spent countless hours in the back yard with Destiny," Mindy Bolen said of her daughter.

Kayla Livingston and her dad Bobby share a special, quiet relationship.

While Todd and Kelbe have a driving force and visibly show their determined attitude to play the game and work hard in an open way, the Livingstons are just as happy to sit back as they are to take the lead.

Bobby Livingston may not be the most vocal, but he may be as consistent as any parent.

"I've pretty much been to every tournament," he said. "It's a lot of miles."

He then began listing the road trips - Little Rock, Sherwood, all over the state of Mississippi, Oklahoma City, Texas . . .

At high school, during local youth league softball and Playmaker games - and practices - Bobby Livingston is there and so is Kayla.

Next to the dugout, along the fence, behind home plate while sitting in the bleachers, Bobby Livingston, looks on, cheers and provides quiet support.

Like her father, Kayla is consistent and omni-present.

You need someone to play third base, there is Kayla. She plays in the outfield and can even pitch. Shortstop and second base are also in her repertoire.

"She doesn't complain," Bobby said. "She'll do whatever she is asked to do. Whatever position you ask her to play, she'll do it."

To be able to fill every position and make the play every time, finding some practice time is mandatory.

"The girls put in a lot of hours themselves," Bobby said. "We hit, we throw."

"When them daddies and daughters get out there," Mindy explained and laughed.

The Playmakers are players, but not always - just most of the time.

On vacation, walking down the halls at school or simply lounging around the house, Jada Wilson does not look like what you would picture as an athlete. Neither is she your typical softball player.

When it is time to play the game or practice a spirit comes over her. She goes after the sport of softball with a one-of-a-kind spirit; it is as if she were a combination of Ernie Banks, Pete Rose and Joe Morgan.

Before practice or after games, Jada's smile lights up a room and she can crack a joke; but, in the dugout during practice or once she moves out on to the field in a game Jada is all about the moment and she takes the moment very seriously.

I have often seen girls playing high school softball - and sometimes college level softball - running out to the field with gloves that seem three to four times too big. The girls carry the glove like a piece of baggage. They also prepare to field ground balls like they are 12-year-olds waiting for a boy to cross the gym floor in order to ask them to dance. They then throw the ball with a loopy arm motion. When the ball is hit up in the air they stumble in an effort to get under the airborne object.

Wilson does none of those things. She is smooth like Banks. She hustles and takes bad hops in stride like Pete Rose; and she makes plays like Joe Morgan when she is around the bag.

Whenever a pitch is made, Wilson is in perfect position to handle the hard hit ground ball or move either to her right or left as an infielder. Should the ball fly up in the air, Wilson is there when it comes down.

"She played with the boys," Tonya Wilson said. "It didn't matter what they did . . . . (even) tackle football."

"Yes, I wanted to do everything the boys did," Jada explained.

Mother Tonya said, "Her very first toy was a squeaky bat and that squeaky ball."

Tonya said she has been around the world with Jada and softball.

"I don't have a life, going to the games" she said with a laugh. "This becomes your family."

But, the conversation soon switched to Jada and her Dad.

"Her daddy has been the sports person."

"My daddy always taught me to play hard," Jada explained. "He taught me never to walk."

She smiled and had a slight laugh as she said, "He worked me to death."

Looking back, Jada's success, which includes her being named All-State as a high school player and competing in All-Star games, is in part tied to her father's role as mentor and first coach.

"My dad as a coach was maybe the best softball thing that has ever happened to me," she said. "I'm a tough kid when it comes to sports because of him.

"He basically taught me to play like a baseball player."

She said she has more than once left the practice field with her Dad cut, bruised, emotional and exhausted.

However, she said that has made her tough and that is a good thing.

Jada Wilson is tough as an athlete, tough-minded as a person and strong enough to handle being an outsider as the only African-American on the team.

She also is very often the only African-American in those championship or prestigious tournaments the Playmakers attend.

"At first she asked why don't I see a lot of people that look like me," her mother explained. "She's adjusted."

Yet, Tonya has admitted that it is tough on the family being the only black family at practice and games. And Jada is aware of that situation.

Additionally, she is often viewed by those who do not know her in a stereotypical fashion. People and opposing coaches think that she is an "African-American" player who uses her speed to get on base or to get to the baseball when playing in the field.

Nothing could be farther from the truth.

"Through all the blood, sweat, tears, bruises and injuries I do not regret being coached by my father," said Wilson. "He is the reason that I'm a great player."

The confident Wilson is definitely tough-minded and her father said she simply never quits.

Asthma may add to her hurdles, but she marches on ahead.

One time a doctor said she should cut back or stay away from sports because of asthma, her father told me.

That advice went in one ear and out the other, as the old saying goes.

Four years of high school basketball combined with prep softball and the Playmakers kept her active. She was so active that she had little vacation time except for a two-week senior trip to Florida with family and friends during one 48-month period - yes, 48 months or four years.

After returning from Florida in June of 2013, Jada's calendar included a college tryout, another high school all-star game and her return to the Playmakers.

On the infield diamond, Jada makes the plays the same way Morgan, Rose and Banks did. She hustles. She is in the right place at the right time because she knows where she has to be when the ball is hit. She can reach base on a bunt or beat out an infield grounder. She also never stops running and often produces hustle hits. Wilson has also been known to crack vicious line drives or hit balls over the fence. All of that comes from being Daddy's girl - and the hours Jada and her Dad spent practicing together - or by playing against the boys.

Jada Wilson plays with a focus on the field that appears to be emotionless or angry. Yet, that is also deceiving.

She can breakdown and find ways to be mischievous in her own unique way.

She plays shortstop for Hamburg High School during the school year and has perfected a move that gets out unsuspecting base runners that start off second base on infield ground balls hit out toward Jada.

She will quickly gobble up the ground ball, take a step or two toward first base and then appear to throw the ball to the first baseman without looking at the runner.

The base runner will then make a move toward third base only to find Wilson standing next to them with the ball. Before the runner can move back to the bag, Wilson makes the tag for an out.

That takes a runner out of scoring position and often angers opposing coaches, who then yell, scream and lose their cool as they berate the hapless baserunner. Hamburg and Wilson get an out and the upper hand in the mind game of softball.

Aubree Head, she plays her high school softball at Crossett High School, knows that move very well.

Earlier in 2013, when Hamburg went to play Crossett, Head was standing at second base as a baserunner. The ball was hit sharply to Wilson. Wilson charged, made the play and looked to first base. However, no throw was made.

Aubree knew what Wilson was doing and stood her ground, never taking her foot off the second base bag.

Aubree looked at Wilson. Wilson smiled back. No out on the play. Meanwhile, howls came from the Hamburg dugout, Hamburg coaches and Hamburg fans. Why didn't Jada throw the ball? What was she doing?

Aubree knew that she had just won a battle with her tricky Playmaker teammate. After the game, Chris Head had the biggest smile one could imagine.

His daughter had just made the right move and won the moment.

"Aubree knew what she was doing, she's done it before," he said.

As for the rest of the inning, Aubree and Jada kept cracking wise and talking to each other. In just a few weeks the high school rivals would be playing together again as Playmakers.

Jada is not unique.

All of the Playmakers know that they are girls off the field, but players between the white lines.

Again that comes from the relationship they have with their fathers.

Makenzie Pierce said her dad lets her play and never comes out to check on her unless he knows she is bleeding.

"We've always had our dads coaching us," Kelbe said. "They coach us like baseball players. They didn't know anything about softball."

Was that a dig? Was that a shot across the bow?

"Ya, like boys," Destiny Bolen said with a laugh.

"We're athletes," Pierce explained about playing with pain and stepping aside only when injuries actually reduce the level of performance.

She said that she does not like to sit or be replaced with a pinch-runner.

She admitted that she is the slowest member of her very athletic Playmaker family, but she knows how to run the bases.

Then there is the intense yelling that comes with playing for coaches that demand the best.

"If they don't yell at us they don't love us," Aubree said of the determined voices belonging to their dads.

Todd may beg to differ.

He moved to coaching the Playmakers after coaching boys.

"I threw a fit," he said about his first practice session with the girls. The girls, he explained, began crying and he knew right then that his daughter's team was going to require an adjustment after he had spent several years coaching Kelbe's brother Conner.

"You coach them like boys, but you treat them like girls," he said. "You treat them like your own."

Still . . .

"We expect the hollering," Kelbe added, before Livingston said, "tough coaching has made us the team we are."

"The only thing I demand out of the kids is to hustle," Coach Callaway said with a grin following another game and another win as his daughter walked past.

"It doesn't take skill to hustle."

It must have been the one time Kelbe did not listen to Coach Callaway as she simply walked on past.

Katie Koen and her father, Brad, "spent countless hours," together working on "ball."

She said she always wanted a pitching machine and when she got it that made her day and her life.

"She started off as a pitcher," Brad Koen said. "We realized at T-Ball (that) she was going to play ball."

Koen said that she started at 6-years old, got involved in "travel ball at 10" and will continue playing after the Playmakers break-up because she will attend the University of Arkansas-Monticello on a softball scholarship.

As she talked, Brad stood by proudly. One of his favorite photos is of him and his girl hugging after a game.

I asked if it is tough working for a tough taskmaster like her father. Katie looked at me as if I might have asked something in a foreign language.

Then she simply said, "He's my best friend."

Destiny Bolen plays in the field.

Aubree Head fields a bouncing ball at shortstop.

INNING THREE

I first ran into the Playmakers on a Monday night when I was on my way to a Hamburg City Council meeting. Yes, I really do work for a living by writing for a weekly newspaper in Crossett, one that covers Ashley County, Arkansas.

Hamburg is the county seat, and as I was headed to the charming southern village that features a classic downtown and way too typical city square I drove down Highway 425. As I drove and entered Hamburg city limits, on my right was a large house set well off the road. It had a well manicured lawn. It had a long driveway. It also had this very large white sign saying welcome home to the Playmakers.

I made a promise to myself that I would check it out on my way back to the office.

An hour later, after the meeting had ended, I was driving back and saw the sign.

I pulled my car over and parked in the driveway.

Knocking on the door, I introduced myself to the elderly woman that met me on the stoop. It was Kelbe's grandmother. Callaway cousins came out of the house and a phone call brought a young lady with red hair and a quirky smile. It was a smile that clearly lit up a darkening night sky.

I snapped a picture of a beaming Kelbe with family and a friend or two in front of the sign.

That was the beginning.

It was a year after I had heard about a softball team from Arkansas.

The summer of 2010 was my last summer working for a paper in Wiggins, Ms.

It was during that summer that the local Stone County team from Wiggins was invited to play in a regional tournament in Arkansas.

Upon the team's return, word spread about how good Arkansas softball is and about a championship team from The Natural State.

Turn the clock forward to 2011 and that team from Arkansas went down to coastal Mississippi for a regional tournament.

Rain plagued the competition, but the Playmakers found a way to beat a team from Texas. The tournament victory sent the Playmakers to the World Series.

Because of the rain, the tournament ended on the Monday of my drive.

The sign was put up immediately - and just before my drive to Hamburg.

Being new to Arkansas I was unsure how I would be treated when I walked up to the front door.

Yet, the Callaway family simply treated me as if I were someone they had known for a long time.

Kelbe was like a young cousin I had not seen in years and she had to tell me about the championship.

That became the norm, I learned, when one dealt with a Playmaker family.

The next day I arranged to get with the team for a team picture with the team trophy they won in Mississippi.

I had left southern Mississippi less than three months before.

It seemed there was some trick with fate, much like a movie. I was in Mississippi when the Playmakers were playing for a regional championship in Arkansas. I moved to Arkansas and the Playmakers were playing in Mississippi. But fate would have to wait.

During the Tuesday photo op with the entire team I met a special person - Lissa Pierce.

There are people that are special and the Playmakers have many special people. But, Miss Lissa (Makenzie's mom) was really unique.

In the South it is common to call people by their first name preceded by a Mr. or Miss.

I may have been called Mr. Robert many times before stopping to realize it. But, once I did the Southern custom became second nature to me.

At the photo op a lady came over to me and introduced herself to me, her name was Lissa Pierce.

"Mr. Robert," she said without hesitation.

I was trying to get information on the team for my story on its upcoming trip to the Babe Ruth World Series of Softball in Colorado and Lissa was the person I had to meet.

Miss Lissa grabbed my arm and attention. She told me that six of the girls had been playing together since they started playing softball. She said these girls were the original Playmakers.

I then went on to put together a sidebar on those six girls.

From that moment until a fateful day in December, I found a great friend in Miss Lissa.

When I needed a word, she was there with a supporting text or a smile.

The Playmakers, I learned, would not have been if it were not for her.

She was an original coach and the team's managing director.

Miss Lissa will always be Miss Playmaker.

During the World Series trip to Colorado, she must have sensed that the girls were tense. So to break the tension she gave up the title of team mother and chaperone. Instead, she became the team's leading prankster.

"She went around scaring the kids and me with frogs," Mindy Bolen, Destiny's mother, said.

Frogs?

"She would go around, she told me to close my eyes and then she'd put a frog in my hands," Mindy explained.

OK.

I asked the players, and Kelbe said that was true. Here was one of the mothers, according to Kelbe, "throwing frogs at everybody."

The girls said she got Jada real good "with two frogs."

Before there were the Playmakers, Kelbe and Makenzie were teammates on a small youth softball team that played in a league that moved from T-Ball to one using a pitching machine.

"Mom and Miss Lissa started us off with the pitching machine," said Kelbe.

Lissa Pierce then moved off the field as the coaching duties were taken over by the Dads.

"She was the team mom everybody looked up to, cared about," Kelbe said. "Our team mom."

Jada Wilson agreed.

"She was our softball team mom."

When the Playmakers were being put together, Aubree Head was an outsider because she was not from Hamburg. That did not last long.

"She invited me over to spend the night," Aubree said. That was all it took. Makenzie now had a tall, blonde sister.

"She would sit next to the dugout on a bucket and yell at the coaches, theirs and ours," Aubree said of her new "mom."

She was the team's scorekeeper. She arranged for all of the team's trips.

"She was like a second mom to me," said Kayla Livingston. "She always kept us laughing, never a dull moment."

"She was a mom to me. She was my first grade teacher," Kelbe added.

Kelbe said she'd spend countless summer nights at Makenzie's house, along with other Playmakers.

One tradition that the girls remembered about those evenings involved toilet paper.

Growing up in New Orleans like I did, rolling a house was not considered the proper thing to do. We as kids always did it, but our parents, school officials and the families that got rolled, and the police, never seemed to understand.

Rolling is the art of taking rolls of toilet paper, pulling out a few sheets and then tossing it so that the rolls would fly and paper tails would extend. The rolls of paper would decorate trees, bushes, the roofs and eves of houses and anything else that was high and up in the air.

You would roll houses of kids from other schools, kids you just didn't like for any reason or the teacher that gave you a bad grade - or the property of some adult that made your life difficult.

It was not designed to be something parents or adults would approve of, but try telling that to Miss Lissa.

"She would take us rolling," Aubree said with a slight smile that became quizzical after looking at my face.

An adult leading young girls on a rolling expedition?

Kelbe explained to me, and so did Aubree, that it was a Pierce ritual. In fact if a house was not rolled by Miss Lissa and the Playmaker girls then it was a sign of disapproval.

I was told that most of the houses were owned by Miss Lissa's kinfolk and that everyone enjoyed the escapades.

At this point I should say that Miss Lissa had some inner demons and took her own life.

She was a friend to me. She kept me up when I would need a person to talk to and was beloved by all of Hamburg.

When they held her visitation on a cold December night in Hamburg after her death, the line of people stretched outside the funeral home, down the street and around the block.

She touched so many people and left a legacy that will always be special to anyone who knew her as a friend, teacher, coach and team mom.

After the Playmakers returned from the World Series in Colorado, team rings were handed out after having been designed by Miss Lissa.

Brad Koen said Miss Lissa's death brought the team together. It also was an event that made the Playmakers different.

Like the New York Yankees of the 1970s after the death of Thurman Munson, the Playmakers seemed to become a more serious squad.

The joy that followed the team's regional tournament win in Mississippi and triumphant return to Hamburg and adjacent communities was replaced with a seriousness of tone when the squad won the 2012 regionals in Louisiana. The ensuing trip to North Carolina for another World Series did not have Miss Lissa.

It was not about experiencing the moment; it was about winning - winning a tournament for the team and for its team mother.

When the Sportsmanship Award was handed out back in Luling, La. after the Playmakers ran through the 2012 regional tournament without a loss or a close contest, there was only one player considered - Makenzie Pierce.

The tremendous run through the regional tournament gave the team a strong feeling, and that feeling continued through a long week of World Series games that ended with a Final Four loss. Fourth place was the final result in North Carolina, but the girls felt like they proved themselves at the World Series and proved they deserved to play with the best in the country for the second consecutive season.

But back to Miss Lissa, and her legacy.

During the summer of 2012 and again in 2013, the Hamburg youth softball association invited teams from neighboring communities to compete in the Lissa Pierce Memorial Tournament. Funds raised go toward a college scholarship for a senior member of the Hamburg High School softball team.

The first Playmaker to get the scholarship was Jada Wilson. And since the tournament honors the memory of Lissa Pierce, it is fitting that the championship trophies in the various age groups are presented by Makenzie.

Since this book is being written in 2013, all I can say is that plans are to make the Memorial tournament an annual event.

After Miss Lissa's death, Coach Chris Head evolved into the team's road manager - scheduling games and planning the trips. He has taken over the role of chief cheerleader. Yet, as he once said to me, "there will never be another Lissa."

Destiny Bolen slides home to score a run for her high school team.

Aubree Head, Kelbe Callaway and Makenzie Pierce as
young Playmakers and then as older Playmakers.

INNING FOUR

The Playmakers are based in a small town called Hamburg, Ark., and that has made a big difference.

The Original Six call Ashley County home, with four being actual Hamburg residents and five attending Hamburg High School.

One of the 'Six' - Aubree Head - will always bleed the Maroon of Crossett High.

Koen, Smith and White are from similarly small-town and rural adjacent communities - DeWitt and Monticello - and when a 10th Playmaker was needed for the final season, up stepped Crossett's Avery Barnett to volunteer her talents.

So because the Playmakers are small town ladies from a corner of southeastern Arkansas that puts family and faith atop the list of things that are important, the team has developed an honest and purely regional feel.

It is hard to find streets without a church on them in Crossett and most of Hamburg.

The town that has adopted the girls as their own, Hamburg, is an authentic small, southern town that treasures its Arkansas roots, culture and history.

The town is proud of those that left its city limits to go on to do great things such as win the Miss Teen USA title in Mobile, Ala., play on the championship Chicago Bulls teams during the Michael Jordan era, make it in the world of big-time college athletics or compete in youth World Series baseball and softball tournaments.

Hamburg is a town that has a special love for everything purple because Hamburg High's school colors are purple and white.

Whenever it is homecoming week, the town celebrates with a week of events, parties and parades.

It is called "Paint the Town Purple Week."

Down the road is arch-rival Crossett (maroon and white) and across the county line are the Billies of Monticello wearing bright blue.

So if you want a team that brings Ashley County together and opens the door to players from neighboring Monticello the choice of Kelly green and black makes sense. Any hint of purple, maroon or blue might just lead to a fight among those that come together to root on the Playmakers.

They may call Hamburg their home base; however, the Playmakers want to be known as the team that represents southeastern Arkansas. Everyone else from outside this corner of the world is simply a foreigner - someone to treat with southern charm and respect but still not part of what makes the Arkansas Delta special.

However, choosing a color or hometown was not on the minds of those parents that wanted their daughters to play together on a softball team called the Playmakers - a team that was free of local politics. They wanted to have a team that could travel and win.

The parents had to get along and the girls had to feel like each of their teammates was a sister.

The first Playmakers' team had girls from Crossett, Hamburg and the hamlet called Fountain Hill just a few minutes from Hamburg.

Hamburg was chosen as the team's home because it had a place for it to practice.

Soon, Hamburg adopted the team. It would be their team.

Still, a color was needed and green it would be.

While Hamburg is a proud town, it also has a history. That history included a decision that pushed Crossett forward and led Hamburg to become better known as the county's farm town - the place farmers went to shop and the place where the seat of government was located.

Yet, it would always be in the shadow of Crossett.

Crossett became the big city for Ashley County residents, while Hamburg was the small, country town with a courthouse.

What happened?

The story is best told in the book, "Wilderness Lady," by John W. Buckner.

Crossett was founded primarily as a mill town designed to turn the timber of the region into lumber, pulp products and paper.

In his preface, Buckner wrote, "Capt. Gates thought of building his mill in Hamburg, but became disappointed with the attitude of the people and moved west 13 miles and built in the bare wilderness a town that soon outstripped the county seat in many ways."

Later on in his work, Buckner wrote, "however, when the Crossett Company made definite plans to locate the mill at Hamburg they found it impossible to secure land and the consent of the leading citizens.

"The city leaders of Hamburg decided that they did not want an additional sawmill and refused to sell a location for the mill."

Well, the mill that was born in 1901 - a mill that grew and became Crossett Industries - became the mill that would last. It eventually turned into the home of one of the largest manufacturing operations of the Georgia Pacific family; and the town that grew up around "the mill" became the economic engine for Ashley County. The mill town was named Crossett.

Crossett and Hamburg spent most of the 20th century in a feud. It seemed that because of the decision and the growth of the Crossett mill, the older Hamburg community was forever looking up at the more-populous Crossett.

What one had, the other had to have and the battle continued into the 21st century.

Both towns have their own equestrian arenas, fair grounds, riding clubs, chambers of commerce, rodeos, civic fairs and school systems.

Wearing purple to a Crossett High activity is akin to a death wish. Wearing maroon is a major offense to those in Hamburg.

If Crossett hosts an event, then Hamburg has to have its time in the sun. The same can be said for Crossett when Hamburg leads the way.

There are no tickets or seats left when Crossett and Hamburg high schools play each other in football or basketball.

I covered a youth baseball tournament during my first summer as a reporter for the *Ashley News Observer*, and early round games drew mostly parents and a few other relatives. Then the team from Crossett played Hamburg. Those attending were not just family or friends, they were residents without a direct tie to any of the players or coaches. All they knew or cared about was that it was Crossett versus Hamburg, and it was a ballgame.

It was a battle for pride. It was Crossett vs. Hamburg.

What had been a sparsely filled parking lot earlier in the day soon became overrun with cars and pick-up trucks and bikes. Very little space was left by the time the first pitch was tossed.

When Crossett faces Hamburg in high school football the two communities turn into opposing camps much like Sparta and Athens or Tuscaloosa, Al. and Baton Rouge, La.

High school softball is no different.

"I still want to beat them," Kelbe Callaway said when her Hamburg team plays Aubree Head's Crossett team.

"Braggin' rights," she explained.

Chris Head wants them for CHS; unfortunately he has not been able to find them. In recent years, Hamburg has outscored Crossett in softball - game after game.

Confrontations between coaches, fans and umpires are par for the course when the Crossett Lady Eagles play the Hamburg Lady Lions.

It often seems the only players with a realistic and relaxed attitude in the arena are Jada Wilson and Aubree Head.

Head simply said she relaxes when Crossett and Hamburg play, explaining that she likes talking to Jada when she is on base and Jada is in the field or vice versa. She also shares large and knowing smiles when she stands next to Kelbe on the field of play or on the sidelines after the contest.

That would have to be enough, because hugs and friendship would only happen once the game is over - for everyone involved including players the game has to be played and a winner has to be crowned.

The rivalry between the communities is hard to ignore.

As Crossett became the economic engine because of the steady growth of the Georgia Pacific mill, it acquired the county's only McDonald's, the singular major hotel (The Ashley Inn), the county's only Pizza Hut, the only Attwood's and Brookshires. The hospital - Ashley County Medical Center - and Wal-Mart also located their facilities in Crossett - not Hamburg.

Hamburg clearly needed something Crossett could not match, and that is where the Playmakers come in and add to their story.

When the Playmakers began to grow up and return to Ashley County with tournament trophies in addition to state and regional titles, Hamburg made sure that the team in green and black was as much the town's team as it was the county's team or a team from southeastern Arkansas.

Hamburg Mayor Dane Weindorf made sure I got to meet Coach Johnny Pierce - a leading resident and businessman in Hamburg. Hamburg had something Crossett did not have and could not have - a World Series team.

Just days after the Playmakers won a regional tournament in coastal Mississippi and prepared to go to the 2011 World Series in Colorado, the Hamburg Chamber of Commerce put together a dinner to honor the team. Mayor Weindorf did his part by giving the team a key to the city.

The girls were given the chance to sit on a stage at the dinner as honorees.

The radio station that broadcasts Hamburg High athletics also broadcasted the World Series.

In 2012, the same station broadcast both the southwest regional tournament and the World Series in North Carolina after a fundraiser held in Hamburg. The girls' were Hamburg's championship team much like the Razorbacks represent Arkansas and the Crimson Tide stands for Alabama.

Hamburg is a small town and Aubree said, "In Hamburg everybody knows each other."

She also said the town's willingness to support the Playmakers added to the team's desire to win.

"We wanted to be the big team," she said; and they accomplished that dream. Celebrating alongside the girls was the town of Hamburg.

As the players drove home with their parents from the 2011 16-and-under Babe Ruth Association regional tournament in Mississippi as champions they knew they were going to the 2011 World Series. What the players did not know was what Hamburg was doing in their honor.

What the town did was to get out some paint and put up handmade welcome home signs. Signs were on the lawns of houses along the highway, signs that said, "Welcome Home Playmakers, Welcome Home Champions."

Todd Callaway said his daughter does not get emotional, but she had a tear in her eye - maybe both eyes - upon her return as she saw the signs.

Even after the team fell short of a national title in Colorado, signs on lawns across the rural town said welcome home "World Series" Playmakers.

"The town of Hamburg is so amazing," Kelbe said.

"I'd never ever thought I'd know so many people. Whenever I go somewhere in Hamburg . . . ," Aubree added. "The town was so proud when we came back."

Kelbe said she gets a special feeling when the next generation of softball players in the Hamburg youth leagues yell, "Rally on two, Rally on two like the Playmakers Do."

"(It is great) to be someone others look up to," Kelbe said, adding that it is "sweet."

"Girls come up and say they want to be a Playmaker."

She said there is a special pride in knowing that her team "really set Hamburg on the map."

Because of the team's championship performances in tournaments across the country, communities in Colorado, Mississippi, Texas, Louisiana, Oklahoma and northern Arkansas - as well as teams and families from across the country that faced the Playmakers - now know there is a small town called Hamburg and that it is the home of the Arkansas Playmakers.

"We tell them the town of Hamburg is in south Arkansas," Kelbe said.

"We really set Hamburg on the map."

Is there a difference between high school softball and playing for the Playmakers?

"In summer ball we have a lot more people supporting (us)," Kelbe said.

The annual Lissa Pierce Memorial Tournament is an example of the way Hamburg has adopted the Playmakers and how the Playmakers help the community by doing their bit to support the youth softball program.

Whenever the Playmakers get a chance they will spend an evening at the local city park watching future stars learn the game. As they watch, the future stars of softball try to mimic their heroes.

Today, during the spring and summer months, girls playing softball is no longer an activity for the few in Hamburg.

In a small, rural and conservative town that celebrates the traditional sports of baseball and football, softball is now a major sport - an activity that draws plenty of attention. And it is that way because of the Playmakers.

By the way, I understand Crossett has been attempting to develop its own Playmaker brand as the rivalry continues. I'll keep an eye on the town's progress.

Kelbe Callawy consoles Aubree Head after a high school game during which
Kelbe's Hamburg team beat Aubree's Crossett team in extra innings.

Kayla Livingston (left) and Kelbe Callaway have a
good time at a pizza restaurant in Texas.

INNING FIVE

Working together and playing together has created a unique bond among the Playmakers.

It has also created an attitude that when they come together they rarely lose.

The Playmakers are proud.

Kelbe Callaway is not shy about saying the team is an all-star team and that it could beat any high school team in Arkansas or any all-star team on any day on any field.

All 10 Playmakers attended four high schools in the same southeastern Arkansas league, and nine of the 10 players on the final Playmaker team were within two years of age from each other when the final season began. It is a tight unit that grew up playing and having fun together.

The youngest and newest (three years younger than the oldest team members), Avery Barnett, joined the nine returning players for the team's first practice of 2013 and was clearly nervous.

When they get together on a diamond, they are gregarious teammates that chatter, call each other out and practice with a mission.

"We know how to get under each other's skin," Jada Wilson said.

On one drill the infield is expected to rotate the ball among all fielders with some lively chatter.

Barnett was not expecting the ball as she stood at third base, but it came in lightening fashion just missing her head by inches.

Coach Johnny Pierce quickly explained the drill and the girls all came to her to show their support.

Still, the next ball was thrown to her with the same intensity letting Avery know that everyone was there to improve and to play serious softball. It was also a message that to play with the Playmakers you better get with the program, loosen up and be ready for anything. There are no free moments.

Wilson said the team has no cliques and when asked if she has someone special she confides in on the team, she replied, "Everyone is my closest," and that there are no breaks in the Playmaker bond.

She said the girls on the team are sisters and they are family.

Coach Pierce had a concerned look on his face during segments of the first practice, and after it he quietly said he wondered if the newest and youngest Playmaker could make it.

Fellow coach and parent Chris Head said he thought she could hang and would be OK.

By the second week of league play Barnett was calm and one would not believe she was a rookie - and by three years the youngest on the team.

Smiling, Barnett soon handled the drills as well as the pressure of playing the game with aplomb.

As the summer went on, Avery would get upset that she failed to field a grounder. She had that Playmaker look. After one practice Coach Chris

Head grabbed Avery around the head and told her to relax . . . and that everybody makes mistakes and no one is perfect. She must have smiled for a bit in order to get free of the headlock. She then jogged over to her mom and younger sister. Practice was finished for another day.

After the third week of league games, her mother said Avery was just getting over a serious bout with kidney stones in the days before the first practice and initial set of games - and was not herself. What took place later was the real Avery Barnett.

With support from a positive Coach Chris - and plenty of encouragement from her new friends including that given through the use of modern texting technology - Barnett had calmed down as Coach Pierce began to forget that his young third baseman and left fielder was a rookie.

Chris said she just needed time to see that everyone on the team is family.

"Avery came into the team and she fit in perfectly," Aubree Head said. "Everybody loves her; she is one of the sweetest people I know."

"We all get along," Mindy Bolen, Destiny's mom, said. "We've been together so long, we're like family."

Brad Koen said he knew Coach Pierce because he played for him when he was younger.

Yet, his daughter Katie did not bring her constant smile to the Playmakers until 2011.

Each year the Playmakers look to add a player or two to the basic roster.

The 2011 season was Year Six for the Playmakers and the Original Six was looking to fill out the roster with several newbies. Katie Koen was one of them.

Robert A. Jackson

Two years later as the final chapter of the Playmakers began; Katie Koen had developed into a true part of the Playmaker family brood.

She was brought in by Coach Pierce after he watched his daughter's high school team play DeWitt High.

Makenzie was a freshman at Hamburg High along with Destiny and Kelbe. Jada was a sophomore.

DeWitt won the game, but it was the play of visiting Katie in the field and her hitting (3-for-3) that convinced Daddy Pierce to take off his Hamburg parent cap and put on his Playmaker coaching derby.

Katie was playing on the Arkansas Hustle team when she was not with her DeWitt High team; however, she was the youngest player on the Hustle and it was also in the process of breaking apart.

Looking at the future and a move to a team composed of players closer to her own age, the decision came down to family - her family.

Brad Koen felt comfortable with Coach Pierce, as did Katie; still, the final selling point was the relationship of the players to each other.

"I never had a problem meeting new people," she explained; but added, "They took me in like family.

"This was the first team I played with, that outside ball that I'd spend time with."

"She never played with a team that's as gritty and this team's gritty," Brad said.

To get to Hamburg from DeWitt for practices requires a 90-minute drive as long as there are no road blocks or slow moving International Harvester Combines in the way.

Brad said he has no problem with the drive, in fact he is happy to do what is needed in order to have his daughter on the right team.

"I want Katie to play on a quality team, be on quality team with a quality coach."

Katie began T-Ball at age six, started travel-team ball at 10 and became a Playmaker at 15.

It is easy to pick out Brad at Playmaker games with his infectious and gregarious personality as he yells for and at Katie. He also has his I-Pad that he uses to compile stats, chart plays and keep the scorebook.

He knows that Katie is where she should be as she wears the Kelly green and black of the Playmakers.

Katie Koen played basketball for DeWitt High and when the Lady Dragons would play one of the schools of a fellow Playmaker it would be as if a class reunion was on the schedule.

Girls play before the boys in high school basketball, so Katie would spend the boys' game sitting with her Playmaker sisters.

In the stands during the DeWitt-Crossett boys' high school game, Katie and Aubree hung out and caught up on the latest news.

It was Kelbe and Katie in the bleachers when Dewitt faced Hamburg.

Similar scenes could be found when DeWitt took on Monticello in basketball.

It was May and graduation was in the air. So as Katie Koen walked across the stage in DeWitt, Kelbe was there to cheer along with other members of the Koen clan.

It was not hard to drive 90 minutes to celebrate with one's sister, Kelbe said.

"They (Playmakers players) all came up," Katie Koen said. "That meant a lot."

It is a sisterhood after all.

One fall weekend became a girl's weekend as Aubree, Kelbe, Makenzie, Katie and a couple of the other Playmaker girls slipped away and drove to Fayetteville to take in a Razorback football game.

"You grow up with each other, like brothers and sisters," Bobby Livingston said.

He said every girl has their own personality, but there is no jealousy. Every girl is allowed to be their own person and differences are accepted.

"But, they are all sisters."

Like Kelbe once told me, the team is a team. There are no judgments, just acceptance - and one color, Kelly Green, and one name: The Playmakers.

After late mid-week practices, Katie would often stay in Hamburg with one of the Hamburg Playmakers and drive home the next morning.

"We stay up at each other's house on weekends," Koen explained.

Well, someone must have forgotten to tell Todd Callaway one Wednesday night.

Kelbe's mom was cool with a visit from Katie, but then she left the house as Todd was sleeping.

I guess when you wake up on a late Wednesday evening you do not expect a non-Callaway in the house. Todd got up and walked into the bathroom.

I never asked if he was properly attired or was ready to knock on the bathroom door, but as a storyteller I learned sometimes things are better left to the imagination.

The story of the Playmakers ended with the summer of 2013 because Katie, Ashleigh White and Jada had earned their moving-on papers (AKA diplomas) and were going to college in the fall. Five of the others were going to graduate the following May.

2013 was going to be a swan song of a summer.

Or was it?

Koen and White had earned softball scholarships and were going to the University of Arkansas-Monticello to play college ball.

"I want all of them," Koen said, "to be together again." Yes, Katie Koen had turned the tables. Once recruited to be a Playmaker, she was now recruiting Playmakers to join her at UAM.

Why not stay sisters together in Monticello?

With a year left to make their decisions, Katie's younger Playmaker kin chose to keep their powder dry. Perhaps a chance to play in the SEC or even with everybody's dream team - the Oklahoma Lady Sooners - awaited them? However, family ties are still a tough bond to break with Aubree, Kelbe and Makenzie choosing to take a fall weekend trip to Monticello to check everything out including the softball field.

Coach Pierce said it best.

"They are all on the same page. Nobody on the team was a superstar."

"We all trust each other," quiet Kayla Livingston said.

When Makenzie was absent one day, several Playmakers had the chance to talk about their catcher.

Smiles came, but nothing negative or even a bit naughty.

"Makenzie is competitive. She will let you know how she feels. If there is something wrong she will let you know about it," Kelbe said.

"If she wants to say something she'll say it," Aubree Head said.

But, Kayla had had enough.

She broke down and said "she's very headstrong and stubborn."

According to Kayla, Makenzie will do what she wants, when she wants and why she wants what she wants is very often a mystery.

"Makenzie lets us know," Aubree said.

For Destiny, Makenzie is the one that makes most of the calls when D-Bo pitches.

"She is the best catcher. She always knows what to call."

The catcher-pitcher pairing is important.

Pairs that have confidence in each other bring the best out in each other.

Pierce was behind the plate when Bolen pitched a nearly perfect game during the Babe Ruth regionals in 2012. The pair worked together when Bolen no-hit Crossett High as Hamburg High juniors. The pairing of Bolen and Pierce then led Hamburg High to a conference title, the South Arkansas regional finals and the state semifinals. They advanced together as pitcher-catcher to the state's Junior Classic.

Looking on from her Hamburg High perch at first base was Callaway with Wilson at shortstop and Livingston in the outfield. However, do not tell the trio that they were simply looking on - at least do not tell fans of Hamburg High softball - as the team moved on to earn a No. 1 computer ranking among the state's high school programs.

When Hamburg High takes the field, opposing teams, fans and parents of opposing players start the chatter . . . . "There are those Playmakers."

In leading Hamburg High to a 30-4 record in 2013, Callaway hit .444 with 32 RBIs. Wilson hit .419 with 19 extra base hits. Livingston had 38 RBIs with a .380 average.

Bolen joined Wilson as an All-State standout and all-star game participant because opposing batters managed to hit just .154 when facing her pitching. She had 183 strikeouts in 157 innings.

The credit, Bolen said with a slight smile, goes to Makenzie. Having named the Ninja Turtle to an All-Conference team, regional high school coaches agree that Pierce is special.

There is true magic in the pairing of Bolen & Pierce, or is it Pierce & Bolen.

Despite being high school rivals, Kayla and Aubree have found that differences in school choice have no place in the Playmaker sisterhood even if Kayla can brag about Hamburg's ability to beat Crossett, Monticello and advance in regional and state playoff competition.

"I have been playing ball with Kayla since I was eight years old, which puts her at seven," Aubree said. "Kayla has always been the youngest, but you would have never known it.

"She's an amazing outfielder and one of the only people in the world I trust to be out there with me.

"Kayla is kind of a quiet person, (but) when she starts to talk she is the funniest one on the team."

Tell that to Kayla and she simply grins, before saying well not much except to mutter "that I'm going to have to say something" to Aubree.

Several of the players have nicknames tied to their given names. Destiny is D-Bo, Kayla is Kayla-Mae and Jada is Jada-Boo. Aubree is Bradley to her mom and a few others (although I call her the Professor because of her knowledge of the game), Kelbe is often called "The Killer" because of the way she swings the bat and Avery is "Hoover" or just "hoove" because of her defensive play.

Makenzie is the "Little Ninja Turtle."

Given that moniker, I wanted to know why?

Just look, I was told and so I did.

Does anyone remember the "Teenage Mutant Ninja Turtles?"

Wearing sunglasses, with her equipment on and a helmet affixed on her head - and an ability to fire the softball as if on a laser to get a lazy or too aggressive base runner - the name is definitely appropriate.

But like all Ninja Turtles, Makenzie has another life.

That life is that of a cheerleader.

While Coach Johnny Pierce would prefer that his daughter spend most of her time and focus on softball, Makenzie puts as much into the sport of cheer as she does softball. How else could you explain the All-American medal around her neck, an invitation to work as an instructor at summer cheerleading camps, her selection as cheer captain for Hamburg High and the opportunity to represent her high school in the Macy's Thanksgiving Day Parade.

Toss in her selection to the Homecoming Court and could Hollywood be next?

For Kelbe, playing first base with an occasional trip to the pitching circle is enough for her.

I asked her if she would like to replace the Ninja Turtle and catch for the Playmakers.

"My dad (would) have a cow," she said loudly. "My mother (would) have a cow."

I learned that while Kelbe dreams of roaming the outfield, Coach Todd wants her at first base.

Therefore, she said, playing first and getting a chance to hit the ball is what she does.

That must be the reason why she is a two-time member of the All-Arkansas State Tournament Team for her performances in state high school playoff games.

The "Killer" is not to be messed with during big games by teammates, coaches and family - not to mention opposing teams.

Still, don't think she is not without a little rascal in her makeup.

As I was working as a photographer during the Hamburg High homecoming parade that wound through the crowd in the small southern town, I hear a voice.

"Hey, Mr. Robert!"

It came from a young lady smiling on a float wearing a cheerleader's uniform.

It was Kelbe.

"No, I'm not joining the dark side," she laughed as she mocked those who seek to bring spirit to ballgames.

Kelbe was simply using the day to have some fun at her softball sister's expense and display her school spirit.

Kelbe also does not want to be blamed for the hotel door that was broken during the team's World Series trip to Colorado.

Neither does Makenzie.

"I was taking a shower," the ninja said.

"The door wouldn't close," Kelbe said before that comment was echoed by her teammates.

After having been somewhat rambunctious and regularly slamming the door to their Colorado motel room, the girls said it was Makenzie's boyfriend Zach who was at fault.

Yes, Zach got up to fix the door, they all agreed.

"It closed," they said after Zach fixed it.

Zach's work did not please the motel manager, so it was left to Coach Pierce to change hats back to Daddy Pierce.

"I don't know why," Kelbe laughed. "It worked."

A trip to a local hardware store by Johnny Pierce and some sweat equity soothed the manager as he fixed the broken door so that it finally closed properly.

During the trip, Makenzie wished all of her problems were handled so easily.

"The flies," she said. "The flies were bad. I went to bed every night with a fly swatter."

That was something Daddy Pierce could not handle or fix. That left it up to the Ninja Turtle.

The Final score: Makenzie Pierce 6, Colorado Flies 0.

Similarly, when opposing teams dare take on the Playmakers the result often ends up in favor of Pierce and her buddies like D-Bo and The Killer.

The Playmaker Family is a family that laughs together, practices together, breaks doors together and wins championships together.

Katie Koen and Aubree Head get together after
their high schools played each other.

Avery Barnett fires a ball to first base.

INNING SIX

Inside families there are often special bonds or ties that involve a pair, a bond that they share that no other can match or break.

In the Playmaker family there is one such bond. It involves an Irish lass and her twin brother.

The siblings are the always engaging Kelbe and her more serious brother Conner Callaway.

Kelbe and Conner play ball; she steps it up in softball and Connor does the same in baseball. They also play first base in their two sports.

The Callaways grew up playing ball and Kelbe admitted they still have a big rivalry that is based in love and pride - and the drive that comes with being quality athletes.

"We still try to outdo each other," she said.

"A big rivalry," Conner said.

If one makes an error or goes hitless they hear about it in a friendly way - on the way home or during the evening dinner or when friends are around.

"If he plays awful I tell him. I'm a straight forward person," Kelbe said.

Batting averages, fielding averages and winning scores are part of the Callaway family conversation - particularly between brother and sister.

Conner is quiet and answers only when asked. Kelbe has the spunk and is willing to step out with a more expansive response unless she is not going to wait for the question - and then you get a sharp statement. Kelbe is not shy.

Kelbe said they work out together, pitch to each other and hit to each other.

Kelbe explained that playing with boys was never hard for her.

"I practiced with boys so I could hit off (both boys and girls)."

She said she worked with boys until she was 12 or in seventh grade.

Admitting that it was hard emotionally and physically - and that she knew she never would be able to play hardball as well as boys as she grew older - she nevertheless said she could do it.

Kelbe smiled when she said that as she grew up she went to a lot of her brother's games with bat and uniform. She went waiting for the coach to make the call in case an extra body was needed.

It never came because, in part, her father did not want her to play, she said.

Her mother, a school teacher, felt it would have been good for her to play organized baseball with the boys; unfortunately, baseball coaches in Hamburg never would find out how good a player Kelbe Callaway would have been.

According to Conner, he wouldn't have minded if she were in the outfield running after fly balls as a teammate. All he would say was that he would be the first baseman and that he did not have any doubts that his sister could have made it happen if given a chance.

Kelbe and Conner admit their sports differ when it comes to hitting. They both explained that hitting a softball requires different skills and reflexes.

"It's a lot different," Kelbe said.

She described the main differences - the closeness of the pitching circle in softball to the batter and the release point of the pitcher in the two sports. Conner added that the movement of a baseball once it leaves the pitcher's hand is an added issue.

Yet, for the most part, Conner sat back as Kelbe explained the pitching and hitting differences.

Conner knows the differences, but Kelbe is the coach.

Conner then said that she can't hit a baseball as if to question her tutorial.

Being a non-player, I wanted Kelbe's expertise. Yet, Conner wanted it put straight that he is the one that has to hit a baseball.

"He can't hit a softball," Kelbe said to clear it up about her skill set.

No response was forthcoming.

Since she has grown up playing softball, Kelbe understands what it is like to play the game. The same can be said for Conner - a career player of baseball since T-ball at the age of 5.

So when Kelbe and Conner talk to each other it is clear that the rivalry is there until one of them notices that they have gone too far and it is time to simply laugh and provide plenty of support.

"Conner is really good," one says.

"She can play," the other answers without expression.

Not only do they practice together, Conner has become the Playmaker's "Fifth Beatle."

"I go out there when I'm needed," he said.

He will run the bases, field balls in the outfield and provide support during practices.

Conner said he grew up around "most of them,"

"I think of them as sisters," he said.

He said he did not mind going to their games, sitting back and watching the Playmakers.

He said all of the girls get along and he gets along with them.

Well, there are those times when the girls are girls, he explained, and then that becomes too much for him.

During some of those times he knows when to slip away and when not to ask questions.

"They are like sisters," he said. "They have family fights. But they get over it quickly. You know, it's girls."

"Our personalities mesh well together," Kelbe said of her softball mates. "We see each other all of the time. We're family."

But when pressed, she admitted to conflicts.

When that happens, she explained, enough space is given so that everything can calm down.

One of the team's parents - Bobby Livingston - quickly agrees.

"There is no hollering or screaming at each other," he said.

During my research for this book, I asked Chris Head about one of the players and he said it's just girls being teen-aged girls.

Since I do not have any daughters I needed his expert advice on the matter as to why they seem to respond differently to situations, responses that do not follow traditional athletic norms.

He told me not to worry because daughters - or young girls - are hard to understand by parents at times. But, instead of talking about his issues he looked elsewhere.

He said with a smile that even Johnny Pierce has told him that he sometimes cannot figure out his daughter when she and her Playmaker sisters sometimes get into that mood - and Johnny has been a coach and father of teens for a long time. If anyone should know, it is wise old Johnny Pierce, Chris Head said with a nod of advice.

When one Playmaker gets quiet everyone gets quiet or when one gets excited everyone gets noisy, and how they get that way is something he or Johnny Pierce cannot explain.

So, maybe Conner is correct when he said, "You know, its girls."

Yes Conner, only the girls really understand each other.

It is a sisterhood of the Playmakers.

It has been that way for eight years.

While Kelbe tells it like it is, she tends to shy away from talking about her influence with younger girls.

She would rather let Conner answer questions about the team's status across the town of Hamburg, and sit back.

"A lot of the younger softball players look up to the Playmakers," he said "I see that a lot."

Kelbe said it is sweet to have young girls look up to her and to Aubree Head, Makenzie Pierce and all of the other Playmakers.

She added there is a lot of responsibility when "kids want to be a Playmaker . . . and view you as a role model."

That is where her most memorable moment comes into play.

Producing the big hit to win a game, a clutch play in the field or explaining how she came up with her desire to find a way to win even when the hour is late, is not her most memorable moment. There were too many hits or fielding plays for the Playmaker gem to recall. Instead she chose Colorado.

She chose a moment that explains why she is a winner.

During the team's first World Series trip, Callaway was handling pitching duties along with that of Destiny Bolen and Bre Smith. She was considered one of the team's aces and Kelbe was looking to help her mates win it all.

But then misfortune stepped up to derail the team and Callaway.

"I hurt my knee," she said. But when pressed about it, she admitted, "I tore my ACL and a torn meniscus. I blew out my ACL."

I asked her how it felt two years later and she said, "What ACL?" She does not have one in her right knee, she laughed.

She knew she had to continue on for her teammates and for her hometown - and high school. So her ability to fight back and rejoin her teammates on the field of play was amazing and impressive.

Her injury happened in August 2011. In hours - just after the incident - she was back in the World Series dugout with a brace over her knee. She also was on her feet, cheering on her sisters. This was much to the chagrin of her coach and vey protective father.

She said she screamed when the knee injury happened, but gave "the hang loose sign" and smiled to her teammates as she was carried off the field.

That did no good, she said, as she saw Aubree and Kayla Livingston crying.

"I don't know why, I was the one that was hurt," she said.

Without Callaway able to pitch or play and lacking Series experience, the Playmakers fell short of the finals.

Callaway wanted to come back and help her Hamburg high school team in 2012 - and the Playmakers. Losing in Colorado was a painful memory. Her goal was to help the Playmakers make it back to the 2012 World Series in North Carolina after leading her high school team to the playoffs. It was a tough task and challenge; but, Conner said she could do it and he was not worried.

She tried to return to the mound, but became a part-time pitcher (when not hitting or playing first base) in high school and a full-time first baseman for the Playmakers because of her knee injury - and the development of the right arm of Destiny Bolen.

Still, returning to the sport so soon was amazing.

With Conner pushing her on with constant but friendly verbal jibes, Kelbe was working out by December. She was in uniform by January and pitched for her high school team in the season-opener in late February - just over seven months after the incident in Colorado. Her Hamburg High team went unbeaten in league play, reached the playoffs and Callaway was named to the state's All-Tournament team for her achievements. The Playmakers were state and regional champions - and finished 4th at the World Series - that summer.

Mention the comeback to Kelbe's parents and they laugh, shake their heads and say that's Kelbe. Meanwhile, Connor simply smiles as if to say that is Kelbe simply trying to get an edge in their rivalry and earn some compassion.

Will that happen? Could that happen?

Conner just grinned and shook his head. I guessed the answer was some form of, "Not on my watch."

The Callaways will do anything to gain an edge, but they will never give up even if they have to climb a major league hurdle.

For that reason, both are winners; but, back to their special bond.

Conner and Kelbe share that special bond and she knows how to get him to carry the load even when he does not want to do it.

Earlier I wrote about the Father's Day Classic that ended at about 3 a.m., according to Kelbe.

"It was ridiculous," she said with a laugh.

Kelbe said she was so worn out that she had to be carried from the field after the Playmakers won. That is a tale her teammates also tell; but, Conner has a different version.

"It was late," he said; then, added that she was just lazy.

"She kept asking me to carry her to the car," he said.

"I was sore for a week," she said in her defense. Then there was her knee injury, which even Coach Todd Callaway would confirm.

Conner said he was tired, too; but, he was her brother and finally he just gave in to the pleadings from a silly sister.

Conner carried Kelbe that morning.

Kelbe also carries Conner, when she has to do it, and makes sure the Playmakers have a brother they can depend upon. Conner is a Playmaker, and if anyone doubts that - just ask Kelbe.

If you doubt her, sit back and listen.

Anything you say Miss Callaway.

Conner sits back quietly. He knows what just happened and he won't help you get out of it. As I turned toward him, he had a slight grin.

Yes, Kelbe and Conner share a bond that only they know about and can explain. So, I guess there are 11 Playmakers and the so-called "Original Six" should be modified to read the "Original Seven."

Yes, anything you say, Miss and Mr. Callaway.

Destiny Bolen pitches for the Playmakers.

Jada Wilson shows that she can smile and enjoy the game.

INNING SEVEN

The 2013 season began with plenty of anticipation. The core of the team - nine players - began their third season together with six having played with each other for at least eight consecutive seasons and one (Bre Smith) was in her fourth year as a Playmaker.

The team had accumulated five state championships, three regional tournament trophies and a pair of World Series trips along with a trove of other trophies and honors during their time together.

Still, 2013 was going to be a challenge. The squad moved up to the 18-and-under classification and left Babe Ruth ball for USSSA.

Coach Chris Head said USSSA offered a greater challenge and would expose the girls to a wider audience - and potential college coaches. It was not a universally approved move, but enough showed support to make the move.

Time also moved forward as all but four of the team's 10 players were going to be juniors or seniors in high school when September rolled around. The parents started to talk about college even if the girls preferred to stay focused on the softball diamond and keeping the Playmaker family together.

Three others were high school graduates, so they could be excused if they turned their focus away from softball and to their move away from home.

It was also going to be a season with several bumps in the road - one was more than a simple bump.

Coach Callaway said it best at the USSSA state tournament when he talked about the season.

"The girls this age, they get cars; and they've been playing ball every summer," he said. "This is the first summer they get to do something other than ball."

He then went to coachspeak.

"They are not getting enough batting practice."

Three of the Playmakers graduated from high school in May. That led to senior trips, graduation parties and senior all-star games.

All of the girls that were getting ready for their senior year of high school also had a chance to play summer all-star games and take trips to out-of-state softball camps to improve their skills and be seen by college scouts with scholarship money.

Practice time suffered, and early in the 2013 season replacement players were brought in to fill holes in the lineup when conflicts arose.

Johnny Pierce looked back and said it was not like it had been in previous years.

The season began with several Tuesday night games in El Dorado, Ark. against high school teams from southeastern Arkansas.

The Playmakers won all five games primarily because of the team's dominant pitching provided by Destiny Bolen and Katie Koen.

The team's hitting was erratic, but it was not needed because opposing batters were routinely handcuffed. Strikeouts, ground balls and routine fly balls were the order of the day whenever Bolen and Koen pitched.

The first tournament was around the corner, and then came the news that Jada Wilson was unable to make the trip to north Arkansas.

A second blow soon followed.

Four days before the trip to Benton, Ark., Coach Chris Head received a call from Aubree. She hurt her hand while playing shortstop at a camp in Tuscaloosa, Ala. Aubree returned home with it bandaged.

It was her throwing hand, so during a Playmaker practice she was placed in the outfield. She couldn't hold a bat but she could wear a glove, catch fly balls and then flip the glove up and grab the ball with her left (glove) hand. Her throw was cut off and relayed back in to the infield.

She said she was ready, but her father Chris was not so sure.

He wanted a doctor's opinion. It came and it was not good news.

The hand was broken and she had to undergo an operation. The tournament began on Saturday; however, on Friday Aubree Head was wearing a cast.

The team travelled north with eight players, but Chris Head displayed his skills as a general manager.

Phone calls the day before the tournament landed a young girl from southwest Arkansas that wanted to play softball - Avery Kesterson.

"Her nickname is 'Big A,'" Brad Koen said, "But, I don't think that has anything to do with her size."

He went on.

"She may weigh 100 pounds soaking wet. However, she plays pretty big."

Kesterson played third base in place of Wilson and was the team's lead-off hitter.

"I've played with many different pick-up players over the years, and I have even been the pick-up player several times before," Katie Koen said.

"Usually they just come in, take care of business and stay separated from the team. (However), 'Big A' fit in just as well as any of the other girls on the team.

"She laughed at all of our silly jokes we tell when we warm up and proved herself worthy to be a Playmaker when she played."

For that reason, the Playmakers displayed the grit that is associated with being a Playmaker.

After opening the tourney in Benton with a 3-2 loss that featured several pitchers and an anemic offense, the Playmakers moved ahead.

"We don't play well in the morning," Pierce said.

Pierce also said, "The other team was just hitting the ball well."

Multiple pitchers were used because Destiny Bolen had a stiff back, Brad Koen explained.

He said, "Coach (Johnny) Pierce pulled Destiny and had her dad, Brian, go to work on her back."

Despite the loss, Katie said, "The entire team was on the fence in the dugout and everyone was cheering. I love how this team rallies around each other."

The rally turned into victories and the trip to northern Arkansas from Hamburg ended up with one tournament down and one tournament trophy for the Arkansas Playmakers.

Bolen returned to the mound after the loss and the team won three consecutive games.

Bolen was not the best pitcher on the team when she was younger, but she developed into a fierce pitcher with an overpowering fastball as she matured. Then when Kelbe Callaway (one of the team's aces when not playing first base) suffered her knee injury in Colorado, Bolen stepped up in the pitching circle. Throughout 2012 and 2013, Bolen's pitching was often the difference between a win and a loss. That allowed Callaway to become a consistent standout at first base and solidified the Playmaker lineup with a single dominator on the mound and a full time first baseman.

A 5-0 tourney win over Ferndale was followed by a 2-1 triumph versus Nitro and then a 3-2 victory over Nitro.

"Destiny was pitching great," Makenzie Pierce said of her battery mate, "and our defense was solid."

Bolen tossed a one-hitter with four strikeouts during the 5-0 victory, while Pierce surprised a base runner leaning the wrong way and picked her off first base.

The offensive attack was led by Kesterson and Kayla Livingston as the pair went 4-for-5 with an RBI.

The win was special because it came against Ferndale, the team that forced the Playmakers into overtime in the marathon match a year ago in the Father's Day Classic.

Having lost its opener, the Playmaker club was forced to top Nitro twice in the finals of a double-elimination competition.

The 2-1 triumph featured another overwhelming effort by Bolen.

Bolen told me once that she played and pitched in a game with a broken arm. Unfortunately for Nitro hitters, nothing bothered her shoulder and her arm was 100 percent.

However, during both games, Nitro felt the wrath of Bolen's bad back.

The high school junior soon to be senior showed why she is the team's heart in the pitcher's circle.

She simply reared back and threw fast ball after fast ball while mixing in what are called off-speed risers and sinkers.

Nitro batters were held to one run on three hits while they swung and missed enough pitches to produce seven strikeouts in the first of the two final round matches.

Frustration for Nitro grew to red-hot proportions when Coach Chris Head noticed that a Nitro player that had left the game for a replacement re-entered in the wrong place in the lineup. In youth softball, players can leave and return, but must return in the same lineup position they were listed in at the start of the game.

The error made by Nitro cost them an out and the player was sent back to the bench.

Nitro fans and coaches were none too pleased and Head became the object of some not so nice language.

"Their coach was livid," Brad Koen said as he looked back on the incident, "and had some choice words for our coaching staff."

Head said he didn't mind and simply was asking that the rules be enforced.

The out came when the contest was tied 1-1 and helped to end an inning with runners in scoring position.

After the Playmakers got two runners on base, Callaway was walked to load the bases. Koen stepped up and she lined the ball through a hole between third base and the shortstop.

It was Koen's only hit, but it was a big one. Scoring was Aubree Head who was used as a pinch-runner, a runner with a cast.

One walk-off hit is acceptable, but the Playmakers faced an angry Nitro team bent on revenge later in the day so more last-inning heroics were going to be needed.

Nitro opened Game Two with a run, the Playmakers then answered.

When Ashleigh White dropped a fly ball in center field, Nitro scored to take a 2-1 edge.

Despite wearing a cast, Aubree Head convinced Playmaker coaches to let her run. It was a moment the Professor of Softball was ready for all day long.

"Not being able to play in a tournament with my team made me feel like I was useless to them," Aubree said. "So when I got the chance to get on base and score winning runs it made me remember what a big part of the team I was. It was great."

After Bolen walked, Head was sent in to run. Bothered by her back, Bolen could use a rest. And needing Bolen in the circle of courage to hold down Nitro hitters, the coaches nodded to Head and she replaced her teammate - the amiable D-Bo - as a runner.

Bolen came back and relaxed on the bench.

Pierce then dropped a bunt that moved Head to second base.

Head looked at home plate and danced off second base, before moving slowly back to the bag. A subsequent pitch got Head leaning off the bag, but the Nitro catcher overthrew her infielder as Head moved back to second.

Head then made a quick decision - she took off for third and did not stop running.

"Aubree went from second to third and she went home, too," Pierce said as if surprised by the girl wearing a cast. The game was tied 2-2.

Bre Smith had three extra base hits in the contest, with the last a triple.

With Smith on base in the seventh inning, the final inning of youth softball games, Callaway did not want Koen to be the only hero. If Koen could end one game with a walk-off hit, she said to herself, then I could do it, too.

"She hit it up the middle," Pierce said, "and Bre scored."

There are no two closer Playmakers than Kelbe and Makenzie.

They grew up together, played ball together, go to school together and celebrate birthdays together.

They share **Facebook** together, hang together, go on double dates together, joke and comment about boys together and win together.

If you want to contact Makenzie, the only person you have to call is Kelbe.

So when Callaway drove in the run, Pierce was there to celebrate and celebrate some more.

Meanwhile, sitting in the dugout with a smile of relief was Bolen.

It was over, finally over. Oh yes, Bolen pitched her third consecutive complete game having allowed two runs and just three hits with seven strikeouts.

Win or lose Bolen smiles, shrugs her shoulders and walks off carrying her bat and gloves alongside her parents.

That brings us to the selection of the tournament's MVP.

Was it Aubree Head for her hustle with a cast? Was it Koen with her hit or Callaway with her single? Was it Bolen?

But, which Bolen? Was it Destiny or was it her Dad and his magic hands as he got his daughter back on the field of play?

Thanks Dad, but it was Destiny's award.

The Playmakers filed their entry fee for the 2013 edition of the Father's Day Classic; but, it was one of those that had to be cancelled. The girls wanted time off and that made the decision to pass it up much easier.

Therefore, the squad approached the 2013 state championship in USSSA having played only once in tournament action.

The team's streak of five Babe Ruth Association state titles was going to be tough to extend to six as the team was the youngest in the field among squads with 18-year-olds across the board. It was also a more competitive USSSA competition.

The Playmakers moved to the 18-and-under class in 2013 when three players became 17-year-olds and kept the squad from playing in the 16-and-under classification.

For youngsters like Avery Barnett, a young lady one month out of her freshman year of high school, and Livingston it was an eye-opening experience.

Going to the suburbs of Little Rock to face teams with several college-age girls was a challenge.

However, since the team had trouble scheduling practices it arrived without enough trips to the batting cages to handle opposing pitchers.

Yet, that was not the team's only handicap.

Kesterson could not make the trip and that forced Chris Head to once again assume the role of general manager.

Jackson

Jada Wilson returned, but Bre Smith received an invite to attend a prestigious summer softball camp in Colorado.

Aubree Head still had her cast and therefore two players were needed to get back to 10.

Brittany McElroy was added as was Taylor Wilson.

Wilson had been a Playmaker before, but after her father died the family moved to Louisiana and Wilson drifted away.

The great GM never loses his Rolodex cards. Chris Head did not lose the card with Taylor's phone number.

Unfortunately, no cards or substitutes or new faces could make up for what happened 48 hours before the start of the state championship tournament.

Destiny Bolen is a tough cookie. She has overcome injuries, she steps up when the moment requires greatness and she goes about her job like a pro.

Yet, it was not a time for anything other than character when her grandfather died 48 hours before the team was going to leave Ashley County for the state tournament.

It was the state tournament and without Bolen the Playmakers had very little hope.

While it was not a moment to dwell upon as Playmakers waited to see what decision Bolen would make, I chose to think about a special time. It was the spring of 2012. It was Crossett vs. Hamburg.

The game was played in primetime and a large, emotional crowd was on-hand to watch the game.

It was the bottom of the seventh inning in Hamburg with Crossett leading by a run.

Bolen stepped up to bat and it was time for the movie called, "The Natural."

Bolen just did not want to lose to Crossett.

She was just a sophomore and sophomores do not make plays like she did; yet, she did.

Everyone on the Crossett team and bench as well as the large Crossett crowd counted down the final outs. Unfortunately, for Crossett, the final out of the seventh inning came too late.

Bolen slapped a single up the middle and did not stop running as the CHS outfielder did not charge the ball. Everyone looked up to see Bolen on second base and she advanced on ground balls to third base and home plate.

The game was tied and went into extra innings. Hamburg would win.

After the game, Crossett fans were naturally upset. Aubree Head, who had smelled victory as a Crossett Lady Eagle, broke down and sobbed as Callaway came over.

Chris Head still has the picture taken of a bereaved daughter being consoled by a Callaway with an expression that seemed to say, "Now come on Aubree, it's only a game."

Flash back over to 2013 and the suburb of Maumelle, Ark. just outside Little Rock.

Bolen stepped up and with her parent's backing played in the USSSA state tournament.

The funeral was on Tuesday. The tournament was played on Saturday. It was time for Bolen to be with her softball sisters.

In Maumelle, she played and pitched for her two families - one of them being the Playmakers. They needed her and she did not let them down.

Kelbe Callaway takes a soft drink break in the dugout.

Katie Koen shares a moment with her best friend and her father, Brad.

INNING EIGHT

I arrived in Maumelle just after the Arkansas Playmakers opened play in the 17-team state USSSA championship softball tournament.

The 18-and under tournament was filled with teams of mostly 17 and 18 year olds, as well as some 19-year-olds who made it because of their birth dates. The Playmakers had a few 17-year-old young ladies, but the rest of the squad was composed of girls ages 15 and 16.

That is what happens when teams move up from one age group to another at state and national competitions, you often, at least for one year, find yourself at the bottom of the age bracket and looking up.

In softball, the biggest difference is found in the pitching. Older girls are not just stronger, they are smarter, more experienced and have more tools.

"USSSA typically has the most competitive state tournament in Arkansas and this year was no exception," Brad Koen said.

Before running into Brad, I met Coach Johnny.

"Go talk to the girls," he said, then added they needed some support.

Makenzie Pierce told me a day earlier that the Playmakers do not play well in the morning.

Well, they opened with a morning game and lost 2-0.

Katie went 2-for-3 and Bolen showed plenty of character in her pitching with seven strikeouts; still, the Fireballs topped the Playmakers, 2-0.

Perhaps the team that lost in the finals of the Father's Day Classic the year before, the epic battle in Sherwood, wanted revenge.

A close call at second base erased Jada Wilson from the basepaths. A pitch that Brad said "was in the dirt" ended up being called a third strike wiping out a Playmaker at the plate.

Instead of two Playmakers standing up safe and alive on first and second base, there were two outs. That meant that ensuing hits by Callaway and Koen came with empty bases and no runners to score.

"One thing about the Playmakers that I have noticed is we are not an early morning team," Brad said. "If we have to play in the morning it takes us a game to warm up."

Only the newly added Taylor Wilson had a smile when I came up. It was clear to me that what the team needed was not a pep talk. What they needed was an afternoon game.

All I can say was that the NWA Chicks was the next team on the schedule and, yes, the game was played after the clock struck noon.

Bolen held the Chicks to one run on two hits with seven strikeouts.

I had asked Bolen about her ability to throw the ball past opposing batters and she once told me that, "it makes me feel bad for them after I strike them out. I always feel sorry for them."

But then why do you do it?

"I like to strike them out. I don't feel that sorry."

For Bolen 14 strikeouts in two games, 14 times where she did not feel that sorry.

Bolen also had two hits vs. the Chicks with one flying well over the left field fence. Her other hit was a double.

Ashleigh White had a double with two RBIs. Wilson had a hit and an RBI. The youngest Playmaker Avery Barnett scored a run. Koen had an RBI.

It was a 6-1 win.

It took two extra innings and plenty of emotion, but the Playmakers beat the Hustle - the same franchise that used to feature a younger Katie Koen - in a mid-afternoon showdown, 5-4.

In this game, Bolen had 10 strikeouts and allowed only two earned runs.

Callaway drove in two runs, Kayla Livingston had a big hit in the first extra inning that drove in a run and both Wilson and White scored runs.

Livingston's hit helped put the Playmakers in front 4-1.

However, a pair of errors enabled the Hustle to tie the game 4-4.

During the contest emotions ran high.

One of the Hustle's three coaches was tossed from the game for constantly griping about various calls by the umpiring crew and Todd Callaway came out of his first base coaching box to argue two pitches that were called strikes - pitches that he thought were clearly balls.

To open the second extra inning, international tie-breaking rules were used. The player that made the final out of the previous inning is placed on second base and action resumes.

The Playmakers had the first at-bat for the second extra inning.

Koen was to be placed at second base, but Chris Head remembered the previous tournament in Benton. He remembered his daughter Aubree.

Unable to hit or throw, Aubree Head knew she could run.

So, did her dad.

During the tournament, Aubree walked to the mound before every inning to stand next to Destiny as she warmed up. She stood or sat at the corner of the dugout when action got underway.

Yet, she still wore a Kelly green cast on her broken right arm. Aubree would have to be the team's cheerleader-in-chief.

That was until her drive to play got her into the game.

Aubree Head is a smart runner and fast. And she once outfoxed the fox - Jada Wilson.

The move was made, Head for Koen.

After some explaining and some pointed questioning by the Hustle staff and fans, with the game tied 4-4, Head took Koen's place.

Bolen came up. She was 1-for-1 with a single. Yet, to the Arkansas Hustle team she was still Destiny Bolen with home run power. They walked her. That would be the mistake that changed the game because you do not walk Destiny or tempt fate.

Up stepped Makenzie Pierce.

Pierce dropped a bunt and a play was made at first base.

Was she out or was she safe, no one knew as the base umpire's ruling was unclear. Head never stopped as she rounded third and charged home.

The ball was thrown home and she was tagged out.

On the play and well after the tag, Aubree was pushed back down once and once again as a scuffle broke out. Coach Head forgot he was Coach Head. All he could see was a catcher standing over his daughter, a young lady with a cast on her arm.

Yelling and screaming, he dashed out to home plate to make his case. At the same time, Pierce left the field for the dugout.

When she reached it and sat down, she was ruled out.

An angry Chris Head was soon followed by an eruption among Playmaker backers.

During the controversy at home plate a time-out was called, Playmaker coaches argued; so Pierce had every right to rest until the game resumed.

Somehow the umpires failed to call timeout.

Pierce should not have left the field. She should have stayed and waited for a clarification of the base umpire's call. Was she safe or was she out? Leaving the field, according to the rulebook, is an automatic out.

Meanwhile, Bolen kept her head and took third base.

The three umpires then ruled three outs and the Hustle left the field.

Well, not quite. There were only two outs and still no time out.

So, Bolen headed for home plate. She scored. Well, not quite.

Huh? The umpires finally called time out to count up to three.

They stopped at two.

Bolen went back to third base. The Hustle then wanted to know how she got to third base. Who was she anyway?

Shouldn't she be out because didn't she leave the field?

"I've been standing here all the time," she said, while coaches and umpires argued.

Destiny simply stayed at third base, except for her attempt to score, and when play resumed Destiny was on the side of the Playmakers and the gods.

The Playmakers were still at-bat, and the winning play was just around the corner.

One wild pitch and Destiny bounced off third base unnerving the lady in the pitcher's circle. Instead of focusing on the batter, all eyes - at least those of the pitcher - were on Destiny.

The decision to walk Destiny was destiny. Another wild pitch and Destiny dashed home to give her team a 5-4 lead.

At this point one incident happened that had a major impact on the Playmakers should be mentioned because it tells us what kind of player Destiny Bolen is once a game begins. Bolen hurt her ankle while running the bases in the win over the Chicks.

She battled through that game and stayed tough versus the Hustle.

But, the long inning and the wait time at third base made her ankle stiffen.

Because of the craziness, no one seemed to notice or ask about her ankle.

Bolen did not mind. The Hustle did and that cost them.

When the Hustle came to bat they put a runner on second base with no one out, per the tiebreaker rule, but Bolen made sure the runner went nowhere.

The Playmakers won 5-4 and it was time to move on to the next game.

Just one more note about the runner. She attempted to steal thinking that Bolen might not be throwing strikes because of her sore ankle and that was a mistake, Bolen fired a strike and the runner was thrown out by Pierce who was ready for action. Pierce's throw was in time but off the bag forcing Jada Wilson to reach out and snag the ball - completing the tag as the young Hustler slid past.

Bum ankle or not, Bolen was ready to pitch; and close game or not, Pierce was ready to throw.

The play was not the only close call defensively for the girls from southeastern Arkansas; but it was a very important play.

During one of the game's middle innings, the Hustle played like they are named.

A baserunner rounded third base on an infield ground ball that was hit up the middle. The Playmakers made the play at first base when Callaway pulled in a throw from Taylor Wilson. Callaway pulled the ball back out of her glove unaware that an opposing baserunner was trying to break a 1-1 tie from second base.

That was until Katie Koen let out a yell. Standing between first and second base, the Playmaker infielder shouted to throw the ball. So did several Playmaker fans.

Callaway fired the ball to Pierce and the runner was tagged out just before she reached the plate with her slide.

In the dugout, Callaway simply said of the hustling Hustler I knew she was going.

She said, with perhaps some of her tongue firmly planted in her cheek, that she baited the hustling Hustler.

Koen smiled. Pierce just said, "I got the out."

She didn't smile until she was sure everyone heard her, and that everyone knew that Makenzie Pierce did the job of blocking the plate and tagging the runner despite being one of the smallest players on the field.

The Playmakers may have survived the Hustle, but the team's hitting woes cost them as the squad realized that pitching and defense may not always be enough to win games.

A team called Intensity was just too intense for the Playmakers.

Bolen saw action as both a pitcher and third baseman in the next contest. At third base she stood her ground and gobbled up every shot hit her way.

However, her pitching finally hit a brick wall. Katie Koen and Taylor Wilson both showed an ability to keep the Arkansas Intensity team from doing serious damage; yet, with two runners on base and Wilson unable to get a ball past a batter after reaching two strikes Playmaker coaches called on Bolen.

Bolen's control left her. She walked two batters and allowed a run to score.

That proved to be enough as Playmaker batters got runners on base, but did not get enough big hits to score more than one run in a 2-1 defeat.

Parents said the girls were tired, out of steam, or they did not have the drive they had when they were younger and hungry.

Kayla had two hits, but both were singles. Every Playmaker hit was a single and that was not enough as the girls fell 2-1.

"It's one of those things," Coach Chris Head said of the move to bring Bolen in to pitch in relief of Taylor Wilson. "It is hindsight. If it works you look like a genius. If it doesn't . . ."

He then talked about the two losses and the team's failure to score runs in those games.

"Definitely, the older pitching had an effect."

He then spoke about the girl's energy.

"I think we left all of our emotion on the other field."

He didn't have to point, it was the field where the Playmakers outfought and outscored the Hustle, 5-4.

Two weeks later, the Playmakers came together for what was likely their final game with the old gang all together. It was the Elite Showcase Tournament in Plano, Texas in mid-July.

The tournament was a showcase, in other words a tournament where college scouts and coaches walked the grounds with pen, notebook, camera and Smartphone.

It was two weeks after the USSSA tournament and Head was healthy enough to play without a cast.

"We played better," Chris Head said.

He said the girls were upbeat and relaxed. They won four of six games and one loss was tied to the requests of college coaches that wanted to see a few Playmakers play different positions and hit different pitchers as they scouted for prospects.

"Aubree did well, she hit .600," her dad said.

He added that Avery Barnett and Kelbe Callaway did well - attracting interest from college scouts.

Still, he did not have to say it but the end was near.

The Playmakers were not playing to win like in the past. They were looking toward the future. The girls without college scholarships were trying out for their future college coaches.

The three seniors - Jada, Katie and Ashleigh - that graduated back in May had their futures lined up. Katie and Ashleigh were going to play college ball at the University of Arkansas-Monticello.

Jada's tryout for Arkansas Tech went well and she was invited to join the team as a non-scholarship player although she said focusing on her classroom studies was her first goal and getting a degree was the primary reason she chose Arkansas Tech. She knew that softball was fun and challenging, but it was not a career and that is why she decided to go to college.

For the other girls, Plano was a chance to get noticed. The handwriting was on the wall and even for Callaway it was closing in on midnight.

Coach Johnny Pierce gives advice to Kayla Livingston.

Playmakers have fun on a bus trip to the World Series in Colorado.

THE FINAL INNING

The Playmakers came together as a team of talented players inside Ashley County. They began travelling across the state and, as Aubree Head told me, "We ate in every Cracker Barrel in Arkansas."

The girls from southeastern Arkansas then set their sights on bigger and better accomplishments.

"We wanted to be the big team," Aubree said.

The Playmakers went outside Arkansas, experienced new worlds and then began to win - and win a lot.

Trips to Tunica in north Mississippi and Gulfport along the Gulf Coast as well as to small towns like Lake Horn were followed by journeys to Shreveport, Cajun country, Oklahoma City, "Big D" and southern Texas. Visits to the Mexican border, the College World Series as enthusiastic and wide-eyed fans as well as to the Rocky Mountains of Colorado gave the young girls a chance to experience what the world is really like. Clearly, they enjoyed the opportunity to broaden their horizons while challenging themselves to be more than just girls from a small corner of rural Arkansas. It was a journey that was well taken.

Kelbe Callaway remembers her first home run in Lake Horn, experiencing the cultural differences found in Deep South Texas, and meeting, getting to know and then becoming friends with girls with different accents and surnames from states like Louisiana, Virginia, North Carolina and New York.

Kayla Livingston remembers that, "We all cried," when the team came back from the first World Series to find that their hometown still loved them despite falling short of the title.

"The town was so proud when we came back," remembered Aubree Head, Callaway and Livingston.

Back in the team's early days Taylor Wilson played two years with the Playmakers before life's turns led her to move to Louisiana.

She then came back when the Playmakers needed her help to fill gaps created by injuries prior to the 2013 USSSA championships. It was like a homecoming, she said, but it also felt as if she had never left. When the state championship tournament ended, Wilson went back to her Louisiana home.

As time passes so do interests.

The 2013 season was the end of Classic Playmaker softball.

Stepping up into a new age bracket and facing stiffer competition in a new association proved to be a very tough proposition for the Playmakers at the 2013 state championships.

The injury to Aubree was just one sign that it was not going to be a year of brilliant memories.

Bre Smith was off to Las Vegas and Canada for skill and college camps. Jada was Arkansas Tech bound as she mixed Playmaker games with her senior class trip, college tryouts and all-star game competition.

Five players travelled to a Junior Classic All-Star Game and then to Alabama for softball camp.

Getting players together for practice was tough and that led the coaches to cut back on tournaments as the summer matured.

Makenzie Pierce wanted to play and she found time to spend a weekend with the Louisiana Blaze.

The team needed a catcher and she stepped up.

"I did well," she said. "It was a blast . . .

"It was a very good weekend for me and I'm glad I was able to go play because it brought my confidence level back up."

A two-run double by Pierce tied one game, sent it into extra innings and sparked a come-from-behind victory. Overall, she finished with four doubles. But it was her arm that impressed those who saw her play as she threw out five runners trying to steal in one game. As word spread about her talent, offers to compete in an all-star, showcase tournament in Georgia found their way to her inbox.

However, Pierce decided that she had enough travel and wanted to finish out the summer with her teammates.

Yet, the final weeks of the summer of 2013 were to be less than special.

After the Playmakers returned from Plano, Texas a serious Katie Koen used social media to announce her retirement from the Playmakers as she turned her attention to life as a college co-ed and collegiate athlete.

Todd Callaway underwent throat surgery and Johnny Pierce had heart surgery.

"I hope it does not come in threes," Coach Chris Head joked.

Kelbe looked at the situation and summed it up as best she could.

"The future of the Playmakers as playing ball wise is unsure; but, one thing we know for certain is whether we're playing ball together or not we'll always be family."

Kelbe posted a **Facebook** picture and it was of her with a girl from a T-ball team in Hamburg. It was symbolic. It was of today's superstar and hero with a young girl that could be the next Kelbe Callaway or Jada Wilson or Katie Koen or Aubree Head.

"If it's our last year together then it's been one heck of a time together. We'll cherish the memories we made and hold onto the friendship as we continue our next chapter," she said, both looking back and forward in time.

Callaway said it would be special if the team could get back for one last shot next summer even if the girls are pulled in different directions - either getting ready for college or preparing for a second year of college life and college softball.

"If we play next year, then that's great, too . . . Next year playing will definitely be for old times' sake. Going and winning tournaments to relive the glory days."

Yet, she explained, hoping for one more summer is something that is natural. For those that have played sports and on one team for as long as they can remember, letting go and moving forward is difficult.

"It will be hard to let go a part of my life that's been with me for almost a decade."

Hard or not, the Playmakers are moving on as Bre Smith and Aubree Head spent the last weeks of the summer of 2013 looking over offers and potential college opportunities.

Callaway and Pierce planned their trips to college campuses. Then an offer to play college softball came for Destiny, an offer that she had to check out.

As summer moved from July to August, Avery Barnett was joined by Aubree in regular visits to the batting cage at Crossett High so they could stay sharp while the Playmaker team was taking August off. It was a chance for them to prepare for their rematch with Hamburg High when school resumed, and play one final time as high school "buddies" against their Playmaker sisters in front of family and friends on the green fields of Ashley County.

Callaway decided that she needed to get ready, too. She made early morning trips to her school's fieldhouse where she went through a weight lifting regimen. She also practiced with her high school team as both a first baseman and outfielder while also drawing questions from the coach who wondered if Kelbe could still pitch.

Pierce found during her August that she was drawn to her final year as captain of the Hamburg High cheerleading squad. Still, she also wanted to stay sharp so she worked out with Hamburg's high school baseball team in the school's conditioning center and field house.

For the five Playmakers that began their final year of high school in Mid-August of 2013, thoughts turned to senior portraits, senior yearbook, homecoming, senior night, one last chance at a high school championship, senior class activities, final exams, the prom and graduation.

For the three Playmakers that found themselves preparing for college, adjustments to a whole new life made the last days of August more than just "The Last of the Summer Wine."

For Avery and Kayla, the focus was on another year of high school and perhaps another year as a Playmaker, should that come to pass.

The month of August neared an end and school was back in session as Labor Day approached. Green jerseys went into storage, replaced with those of purple, maroon and blue.

As for me - and those in Hamburg that found the Playmakers to be our championship team - I'll be like Bogart on the tarmac in "Casablanca."

So to paraphrase his famous line, all I can say is "We'll always have Luling."

For me, a Saturday in rainy Luling, La. will be the ultimate Playmaker moment.

It was late summer in 2012 and the team was the pre-tourney favorite as it sought to both defend its Southwest Regional crown down in Cajun country and return to the World Series in North Carolina.

However, rain washed out opening ceremonies and delayed games.

A flood in neighboring Jefferson Parish kept me from making every game, but the Playmakers kept on and reached the semifinals.

A year earlier the Playmakers had to battle through the regional tournament and fight until the last out to capture a World Series berth.

In 2012 the team was a year older and at the top of the 16-year-old age division. It was also at the top of its game.

Versus Del Rio of Texas, the Playmakers played the semifinal like champions as they finished with 12 hits and simply ran until all four bases had been touched.

A year before a Texas team had nearly ruined the Playmakers World Series dreams at the Gulfport regionals. In Luling, the Playmakers beat their toughest foe 6-0.

Take that Texas, Kelbe yelled.

The bat of Kayla Livingston sparked the offensive performance, but it was a pair of running catches in the outfield that made the night for Destiny Bolen a night of memories.

Bolen was on the mound and she was on her game.

Except for one batter reaching on a walk, Bolen enjoyed perfection as she threw a no-hitter.

I still remember the flashes from phone cameras as Bolen and Pierce held the ball that Bolen threw to strikeout the game's final batter.

In two games that day, Bolen had 20 strikeouts and her achievement made it back to southern Arkansas via social media. However, the achievement was also broadcast as a local radio station had sent equipment with two parents to Luling and they broadcast live Playmaker games back to the homefolks.

With four tourney wins, the Playmakers stayed out of the loser's bracket and had outscored opposing teams from Louisiana and Texas 32-1. The Mississippi state champion simply avoided the girls in green, leaving it to other teams to face Playmaker power.

On Sunday, St. Charles Parish (La.) was the championship game opponent.

Instead of the special moments usually associated with championships, the game had a unique, relaxed feeling.

St. Charles had battled through the loser's bracket of the double-elimination event. Their players were tired as rain-delayed and interrupted games made their route to the finals difficult.

Yet, St. Charles must also have felt like the sacrificial lamb standing in the way of a Big Green Machine, Destiny Bolen and a team that was already talking about North Carolina.

For St. Charles, a 2nd place finish was inevitable.

An anti-climactic air surrounded the field as the sun broke through and south Louisiana heat welcomed the two teams.

St. Charles fielders let routine fly balls fall into outfield gaps. Walks were followed by solid Playmaker hits up the middle - and down the line - and errant throws replaced rain drops. The Playmakers scored often and went on to win 16-0. Every girl in green was a hitting hero.

However easy the win appeared to be for the girls from rural Arkansas, the team did not smile or relax.

For a while, I thought I was watching a team coached by Nick Saban.

Bolen tossed a one-hitter with five strikeouts, errors were non-existent when the team wearing Kelly Green was on the field and hustle was everywhere.

"(The) defense was as good as it gets," Coach Chris Head said.

Yet, let us go back to St. Nick.

Saban has one rule, well he actually has several, but there is one commandment that cannot be breached. You hustle and give 100 percent from the time the first whistle is blown until the game clock reaches 0.00.

Coaches can yell, but in the end they can only watch. The players are the ones that play. They must be the ones to follow the Saban Rule.

Maybe the name Playmakers was chosen because the girls knew what their legacy would be - playing the game with focus until every out has been made and every run is scored.

It was during a middle inning of the championship contest in Luling - the game was in hand at that point - when Bolen gave up a sinking line drive hit to right field.

Well, hold up scorekeepers or as TV analyst Lee Corso has often said, "Not so fast my friend."

Aubree Head was in right field and she charged the ball as it hit the ground.

She picked it up as if she was at shortstop and fired the ball to Kelbe at first base.

The ball beat the runner and another out was registered.

Since the final out had not yet been made, the Playmakers stayed on their toes and refused to let up. A Texas leaguer (a high, shallow pop fly just beyond the grasp of infielders) may turn into a hit against most teams, but on this Sunday morning it was an example of how the Playmakers hustle on every play and every ball that is pitched. Head made the play, but it could easily have been Livingston or Koen or Wilson or Bre Smith. Over the years, every Playmaker has made a similar play.

Bolen's one-hitter held up because no one on her team would give a quarter.

The coaches had to finally tell the girls to slow down, take strikes and remove their foot from the gas pedal.

Saban would be proud that young girls from Arkansas followed his directive without hesitation.

On to North Carolina, and the team continued to battle hard until it was not their night - finishing fourth at the 2012 World Series just one win from the bracket finals.

Still, it was Luling that will stay with me. Bolen won the MVP award and Pierce was given the Sportsmanship Trophy.

It was a shining moment that in the end was just one of many memorable moments for a group of girls that made Ashley County, Arkansas proud; moments that got their fans and families to stand up and cheer game after game and season after season.

Playmakers celebrate with Katie Koen at her high school graduation.

The Playmakers come together wearing their high school uniforms. (This picture was taken before Avery Barnett joined the team as the 10th Playmaker).

Kelbe Callaway drives home a point.